RHYTHM:

An Annotated Bibliography

by

Steven D. Winick

The Scarecrow Press, Inc.
Metuchen, N.J.   1974

Library of Congress Cataloging in Publication Data

Winick, Steven.
    Rhythm: an annotated bibliography.

    1. Musical meter and rhythm--Bibliography.
I. Title.
ML128.L3W53   016.7816'2   74-14582
ISBN 0-8108-0767-X

FOREWORD

Through the years the element of rhythm has been the subject of considerable writing and discussion. Aspects of rhythm have undergone definition numerous times and the pedagogy of rhythmic instruction has been quibbled over ad infinitum. This has all led to the need for a comprehensive look at sources and resources on the subject. Such a "look" needs enough scholarly input as to engage our confidence. This is especially true today, because of the use of widespread generalizations in teaching as well as the typically naive treatment of many musical terms and notational systems in the music teacher's "bag of tricks."

This work is one of the rare attempts to conduct a thorough analysis of rhythm materials. It is an excellent guide for music teachers at all levels, including nearly 500 annotations of books, theses, dissertations, and periodical articles written in English between 1900 and 1972. Certainly, all musicians interested in the precision of masterful teaching will want to use such a reference for the improvement of method and for their general professional expertise.

Sally Monsour
Atlanta

TABLE OF CONTENTS

INTRODUCTION

Erwin H. Schneider and Henry L. Cady, in a recent study of research related to music education, discovered a

> ... lack of an organized body of research information in music education, the need for identifying research studies in a large body of literature, the need for synthesizing knowledges gained from competent research for use in the profession, and [the need for] a system for the dissemination of these knowledges.... [1]

I believe that these deficiencies and needs pertain to research related specifically to rhythm, and that all too often, music educators do not fully utilize the available written materials relating to rhythmic instruction. The problem seems to be either that they are unaware of the existence of much of this literature, or that they find it difficult to extract desired information from such a wealth of material.

This annotated bibliography of selected written materials pertinent to the general background, psychology, and pedagogy of rhythm attempts to aid in solving this problem for music educators and others. Before the development of this bibliography, only two compilations existed that could be considered at all comprehensive.

In the bibliography to Ruckmick's doctoral dissertation, reprinted in the American Journal of Psychology in 1913, with supplements in 1915, 1918, and 1924, [2] over

1

half of the 714 items are in foreign languages. The entries,
none of which are annotated, deal primarily with rhythmical
phenomena in the area of psychology, but also include contributions to the fields of music, pictorial and sculptural art,
prosody, pedagogy, dance, physiology, biology, geology,
physics, and chemistry. The advances made in the field of
music education and the growth of its literature since 1924,
as well as the evolution of rhythmic practices in 20th-century
music, justify an up-to-date examination of the available
materials pertaining to rhythm.

A bibliography of approximately 250 items prepared
by the 1958-1959 Music Education Graduate Seminar at the
Eastman School of Music[3] deals more specifically with materials on rhythm in music than did Ruckmick's. However,
none of the items are annotated, and such areas as the
psychology of rhythm are represented by only a few entries.
Pertinent materials from both of these bibliographies have
been incorporated and annotated in the present study.

The search for suitable books, theses, dissertations,
and periodical articles was conducted primarily at the Sibley
Music Library of the Eastman School of Music. In addition,
visits were made to the Rochester Public Library, Rochester, N.Y.; the Lincoln Center Library for the Performing
Arts, New York, N.Y.; and the Rush Rhees Library of the
University of Rochester, Rochester, N.Y., to insure comprehensive coverage and direct examination of otherwise un-
obtainable items. Book titles applicable to the study were
found in standard references, in the Sibley Music Library's
card catalog, and in bibliographies contained in books,
theses, and dissertations. Thesis and dissertation titles
were obtained from listings in abstracts, from bibliographies

of research studies, and from bibliographies contained in
other materials examined.

Periodical articles on subjects of central concern to
this bibliography range in quality from lengthy monographs
written by experts in the field to brief and superficial discussions based on the often untested opinions of less scholarly
writers. Except for the most flagrant of this latter type, it
was felt that the greatest service would be performed by including most of the applicable periodical literature with the
exception of newspaper articles. The information provided
by the annotations will then enable the reader to decide
whether it will serve his purpose to locate and read any
given entry.

The search for suitable periodical article titles was
undertaken in a manner similar to the search for book,
thesis, and dissertation titles described above. In addition,
general indexes to music periodicals such as the Music Index and the Musical Article Guide, and other indexes to
specific music periodicals have been used to provide coverage as complete and current as possible.

The bibliographies investigated as sources for entries
or annotations follow:

Adkins, Cecil (ed.). Doctoral Dissertations in Musicology.
    5th ed. Philadelphia: American Musicological So-
    ciety, Inc., 1971, 203 p.; supplement in Journal of
    the American Musicological Society, XXIV/3 (Fall
    1971) 414-48.

Besterman, Theodore. A World Bibliography of Bibliogra-
    phies. 3rd ed. 4 vols. (bound in 2). New York:
    Scarecrow Press, Inc., 1955, 5701 p.

Blom, Eric. Music and Letters: Index to Volumes I-XL.
    [1920-1959]. Edited by Jack Westrup. London: Ox-
    University Press, 1962, 140 p.

Borg, Earl R.   A Codified Bibliography of Music Education
    Research at the Master's Level in Selected Institu-
    tions of the North Central Association.   2 vols.
    Volume II: Bibliography and Appendixes [with] Sup-
    plement.   Ph.D. dissertation, Northwestern Univer-
    sity, 1964, 191 p., 401 p.

Ciurczak, Peter L.   The Journal of Aesthetics and Art
    Criticism, 1941-1964 ... An Index of Articles and
    Book Reviews Pertaining to Music....   Emporia, KS:
    Kansas State Teachers College, 1965, 15 p.

Collins, Thomas C. (ed.).   Music Education Materials: A
    Selected, Annotated Bibliography.   Washington, DC:
    Music Educators National Conference, 1968, 174 p.

Darrell, R.D.   Schirmer's Guide to Books on Music and
    Musicians: A Practical Bibliography.   New York:
    G. Schirmer, Inc., 1951, 402 p.

De Lerma, Dominique-René (comp.).   A Selective List of
    Masters' Theses in Musicology.   Compiled for the
    American Musicological Society.   Bloomington, IN:
    Denia Press, 1970, 42 p.

Dissertation Abstracts.   Ann Arbor, MI: University Micro-
    films, Inc. (1938)--XXXII/5A (Nov. 1971).

Dissertation Abstracts International: Retrospective Index.
    [I (1938)--XXIX (June 1969)].   Vol. VII: Education
    and Vol. VIII: Communication/Information/Busi-
    ness/Literature/Fine Arts.   Ann Arbor, MI: Uni-
    versity Microfilms, Inc., 1970.

Duckles, Vincent.   Music Reference and Research Materials:
    An Annotated Bibliography.   2nd ed.   New York:
    Free Press, 1967, 385 p.

Eastman School of Music, Music Education 282 Graduate
    Seminar, 1958-1959.   "Bibliographies of Publications
    on Rhythm."   Rochester, NY, July 12, 1960, 18 p.
    (Dittoed.)

Garretson, Homer E.   An Annotated Bibliography of Written
    Material Pertinent to the Performance of Chamber
    Music for Stringed Instruments.   Ed.D. dissertation,
    University of Illinois, 1961, 91 p.

Goodkind, Herbert K. (comp.). Cumulative Index, 1915 thru 1959, to The Musical Quarterly. New York: Goodkind Indexes, 1960; Supplement, 1960-62, 1963.

Gordon, Roderick D. "Doctoral Dissertations in Music and Music Education, 1957-1963." Journal of Research in Music Education, XII/1 (Spring 1964) 4-112; supplement, 1963-1964, in XIII/1 (Spring 1965) 45-55; supplement, 1964-1965, in XIV/1 (Spring 1966) 45-57; supplement, 1965-1966, in XV/1 (Spring 1967) 41-59.

_____. "Doctoral Dissertations in Music and Music Education, 1963-1967." Journal of Research in Music Education, XVI/2 (Summer 1968) 83-216; supplement, 1967-1968, in XVII/3 (Fall 1969) 316-46; supplement, 1968-1969, in XVIII/3 (Fall 1970) 277-97.

_____. "Doctoral Dissertations in Music and Music Education, 1968-1971." Journal of Research in Music Education, XX/1 (Spring 1972) 2-190

Harding, Rosamond E. M. Origins of Musical Time and Expression. London: Oxford University Press, 1938, 115 p.

Johnson, Merton B. "Bibliography for Conductors of College and Community Orchestras: A Selective Annotated List of Written Materials on Organization, Conducting, and General Interpretive Background." Unpublished D. M. A. dissertation, Eastman School of Music, University of Rochester, 1966, 93 p.

Kinscella, Hazel G. "Americana Index to The Musical Quarterly." Journal of Research in Music Education, VI/2 (Fall 1958) 3-144.

Larson, William S. Bibliography of Research Studies in Music Education, 1932-1948. Rev. ed. Chicago: Music Educators National Conference, Committee on Bibliography of Research Projects and Theses, 1949, 119 p.

_____. "Bibliography of Research Studies in Music Education, 1949-1956." Journal of Research in Music Education, V/2 (Fall 1957) 64-225.

Masters Abstracts. Ann Arbor, MI: University Microfilms,
    Inc. I/1 (1962)--IX/4 (Dec. 1971).

Microcard Publications in Music. Rochester, NY: Univer-
    sity of Rochester Press, Rush Rhees Library, July,
    1965, 20 p.

Mixter, Keith E. General Bibliography for Music Research.
    Detroit Studies in Music Bibliography, No. 4. De-
    troit, MI: Information Service, Inc., 1962, 38 p.

Mursell, James L. "Psychological Research Bearing on
    Music Education." Music Educators Journal, XXII
    (Nov.-Dec. 1935) 24-25.

Music Article Guide: A Comprehensive Quarterly Reference
    Guide to Significant Signed Feature Articles in Ameri-
    can Music Periodicals. Philadelphia: Music Article
    Guide. [I/1] (Winter 1966)--VII/1 (Winter 1971-72).

Music Index: A Subject-Author Guide to Current Music
    Periodical Literature. Detroit, MI: Information
    Coordinators, Inc. I/12 (Dec. 1949)--XXIII/4 (Apr.
    1971).

New York Public Library. Dictionary Catalog of the Music
    Collection. 33 vols. Boston: G.K. Hall, 1964;
    supplement, 1 vol., 1966.

Notes. Ann Arbor, MI: Music Library Association, Inc.
    Second Series I/1 (Dec. 1943)--XXVIII/4 (June 1972).

Paperbound Books in Print: March 1972. New York: R.R.
    Bowker Co., 1972, 2370 p.

Petzold, Robert G. Auditory Perception of Musical Sounds
    by Children in the First Six Grades. U.S. Office
    of Education Cooperative Research Project No. 1051,
    University of Wisconsin, 1966, 277 p.; ED 010 297.

Rahn, D. Jay (ed.). "Masters' Theses in Musicology, First
    Installment." Current Musicology, No. 12 (1971) 7-
    37.

Research in Education. Washington, DC: U.S. Office of
    Education, Education Resources Information Center
    (ERIC). I/1 (Jan. 1966)--VII/4 (Apr. 1972).

RILM Abstracts. Répertoire International de Littérature
    Musicale. New York: International RILM Center,
    City University of New York. I/1 (Jan.-Apr. 1967)--
    IV/1 (Jan.-Apr. 1970).

R. M. A. Research Chronicle. (Royal Musical Association).
    "Register of Theses on Music." No. 3 (1963) 1-25;
    "Amendments and Additions," in No. 4 (1964) 93-
    97; No. 6 (1966) 51-58; and No. 8 (1970) 90-101.

Ruckmick, Christian A. "A Bibliography of Rhythm."
    American Journal of Psychology, XXIV (Oct. 1913)
    508-19; supplement in XXVI (July 1915) 457-59;
    supplement in XXIX (Apr. 1918) 214-18; supplement
    in XXXV (July 1924) 407-13.

Rutan, Harold D. An Annotated Bibliography of Written
    Material Pertinent to the Performance of Brass and
    Percussion Chamber Music. Ed. D. dissertation,
    University of Illinois, 1960, 368 p.

Schneider, Erwin H. and Henry L. Cady. Evaluation and
    Synthesis of Research Studies Relating to Music Edu-
    cation. U. S. Office of Education Cooperative Re-
    search Project E-016, Ohio State University, 1965,
    625 p.; ED 010 298.

Squire, Alan P. An Annotated Bibliography of Written
    Materials Pertinent to the Performance of Woodwind
    Chamber Music. Ed. D. dissertation, University of
    Illinois, 1960, 130 p.

Subject Guide to Books in Print, 1971: An Index to the
    Publishers' Trade List Annual. 2 vols. New York:
    R. R. Bowker Co., 1971, 3588 p.

Vinquist, Mary and Neal Zaslaw (eds.). Performance
    Practice: A Bibliography. New York: W. W. Norton
    & Co., Inc., 1971, 114 p. First published in Current
    Musicology, No. 8 (1969) 6-96; supplement in No.
    10 (1970) 144-72.

Wolf, Arthur S. (comp.). Speculum: An Index of Musically
    Related Articles and Book Reviews [I (1926)--XCIII
    (1968)]. Ann Arbor, MI: Music Library Association,
    1970, 31 p.

Every effort was made to directly examine the materials in the bibliography. Approximately fifty theses and
dissertations were obtained through interlibrary loan; others
were examined in microform.

Wherever possible, book reviews which were judged
to be authoritative, and were published in English language
journals, have been cited or used in part as practical aids
to the evaluation of items. All volumes of the Music Index
available as of June, 1972 (I/12--XXIII/4) were systemati-
cally searched for sources of reviews, as were all volumes
of Notes (Second Series, I/1--XXVIII/4). Other reviews,
especially reviews of study, etude, and method books, were
discovered through perusal of such periodicals as Brass
Quarterly, Brass and Woodwind Quarterly, and the Instrumentalist, and through other less systematic means.

Multiple reviews for single items are listed alpha-
betically by last name of the reviewer at the end of the
annotation. A review cited without the reviewer's name indicates it was unsigned. Reviewers are listed together
with authors and editors in the Index.

In occasional instances where neither the actual
source nor its review could be located, brief annotations
like those in Darrell's Schirmer's Guide ... and excerpts
from abstracts in Dissertation Abstracts, Research in Education, RILM Abstracts, and Schneider and Cady's Evaluation and Synthesis of Research Studies... have been used.

A small number of books and theses not available for
examination have been included without annotation if their
titles seemed sufficiently interesting.

Rhythm is a subject which is inherent in much of the
literature written on music. Which areas related to rhythm

to exclude from the bibliography was a core problem. An evaluation of the annotated bibliographies developed by Garretson, Rutan, and Squire at the University of Illinois, and by Johnson at the Eastman School of Music of the University of Rochester, which are listed above, has suggested the following limitations: historical and musicological works and books on rudiments or fundamentals of music, theory, harmony, composition, conducting, form, and interpretation are for the most part excluded, except where they contain major contributions to the field of rhythm which are of immediate and practical concern to music educators. Also excluded are early tutors, materials on verse or prose rhythm, tests of musical ability, and anthropological research comparing the types of talent that supposedly prevail in various racial groups.

The cursory nature of the foreign language entries in the bibliographies of Garretson, Rutan, and Squire and their complete exclusion from Johnson's bibliography seem to indicate that very little practical value is to be gained by the inclusion of foreign publications, even though much scholarly material exists. For this reason, the present bibliography deals only with materials written in English. [4] With these limitations in mind, the writer has discarded all but 493 of the 1,065 items comprising the bibliography as originally compiled.

The large majority of materials was published between 1900 and 1972. Exceptions have been made for a few historically important works on the description and definition, theory, and psychology of rhythm. While the main purpose of the annotations is to describe the content and point out areas of usefulness, some qualitative evaluation

is included where such judgment seems relevant, feasible,
and justifiable.

Pertinent material was found in such diverse sources
that categorizing the literature was somewhat of a problem
at first. An acceptable compromise was reached which
resulted in categories specific enough to provide a useful
classification and yet general enough to avoid unnecessary
duplication of entries. Each section of the bibliography includes explanatory comments, indicating the extent of inclusion and drawing attention to particularly useful or worth-
while items. Inevitably, some cross referencing was
necessary. For these items, the annotations are placed
in the sections to which they most directly apply, and
references to the annotations are indicated in related sections.

Dissertations available in hard copy or microfilm
from University Microfilms, Inc. (300 N. Zeeb Rd., Ann
Arbor, MI 48106) are listed as published books. Their
entries in the bibliography include the Library of Congress
microfilm numbers used to order the dissertations from
University Microfilms, indicated as LC 58-1329, and the
volume, number, and page location of its abstract in
Dissertation Abstracts, indicated as DA XXXII/5A, 1536.
Similarly, entries for research available in hard copy or
microfiche from the ERIC (Educational Resources Information Center) Document Reproduction Service (operated by
the National Cash Register Co., Microform Systems, 4936
Fairmont Ave., Bethesda, MD 20014) include the ERIC
accession number, indicated as ED 010 243.

The abbreviations used in the bibliography follow:
DA XXXII/5A, 1536   Dissertation Abstracts, Volume XXXII,
                    Number 5A, page 1536.

ED 010 243	ERIC Document Reproduction Service accession number
LC 58-1329	Library of Congress call number for the microfilm of the dissertation
D. M. A.	Doctor of Musical Arts
D. Mus. Ed	Doctor of Music Education
Ed. D.	Doctor of Education
M. A.	Master of Arts
M. M.	Master of Music
M. M. Ed.	Master of Music Education
M. S.	Master of Science
Ph. D.	Doctor of Philosophy

In addition, the following U. S. Postal Service two-letter state abbreviations have been used:

Alabama	AL	Kentucky	KY
Alaska	AK	Louisiana	LA
Arizona	AZ	Maine	ME
Arkansas	AR	Maryland	MD
California	CA	Massachusetts	MA
Canal Zone	CZ	Michigan	MI
Colorado	CO	Minnesota	MN
Connecticut	CT	Mississippi	MS
Delaware	DE	Missouri	MO
D. of C.	DC	Montana	MT
Florida	FL	Nebraska	NE
Georgia	GA	Nevada	NV
Guam	GU	New Hampshire	NH
Hawaii	HI	New Jersey	NJ
Idaho	ID	New Mexico	NM
Illinois	IL	New York	NY
Indiana	IN	North Carolina	NC
Iowa	IA	North Dakota	ND
Kansas	KS	Ohio	OH

Oklahoma	OK	Utah	UT
Oregon	OR	Vermont	VT
Pennsylvania	PA	Virginia	VA
Puerto Rico	PR	Virgin Islands	VI
Rhode Island	RI	Washington	WA
South Carolina	SC	West Virginia	WV
South Dakota	SD	Wisconsin	WI
Tennessee	TN	Wyoming	WY
Texas	TX		

The recent advent of such bibliographic tools as
Research in Education on the national level, and RILM
Abstracts and Dissertation Abstracts International[5] on the
international level makes possible a relatively fast, wide,
and inexpensive dissemination of current knowledge.   This
has resulted in more efficient location, examination, and
compilation of writings pertinent to various areas in the field
of music.

The increased interest in and need for such studies
is illustrated by the dissertations of Garretson, Johnson,
Rutan, and Squire listed above and by current commercial
bibliographic projects.   Scarecrow Press, Inc., Metuchen,
N.J. has undertaken publication of selected bibliographies in
music, and Information Coordinators, Inc., Detroit has a
well-established and growing series of bibliographic studies
entitled Detroit Studies in Music Bibliography, with twenty-
one bibliographies published and six accepted for future publication as of June, 1972.

It is hoped that the present bibliography will serve a
useful function in aiding music educators and others to dis-
cover, evaluate, and utilize the voluminous literature pertaining to rhythm, and in so doing, will effect an improvement in their skill at teaching rhythm and thereby improve
the rhythmic performance of their students.

Notes

1. Erwin H. Schneider and Henry L. Cady, Evaluation and
   Synthesis of Research Studies Relating to Music Education (U. S. Office of Education Cooperative Research
   Project E-016, Ohio State University, 1965; ED 010
   298), p. 6.

2. Christian A. Ruckmick, "A Bibliography of Rhythm, "
   American Journal of Psychology, XXIV (Oct. 1913)
   508-19; supplement in XXVI (July 1915) 457-59; supplement in XXIX (Apr. 1918) 214-18; supplement in
   XXXV (July 1924) 407-13.

3. Eastman School of Music, Music Education 282 Graduate
   Seminar, 1958-1959, "Bibliographies of Publications
   on Rhythm, " Rochester, N. Y. , July 12, 1960, 18 pp.
   (Dittoed.)

4. A bibliography published as "News of Research: Research in England, " Journal of Research in Music
   Education, XVII/2 (Summer 1969) 252-55, compiled
   by Arnold Bentley, University of Reading, of fifty-
   three research studies that have been presented for
   higher degrees in the United Kingdom since 1920 in
   the area of music contains three studies pertaining to
   rhythm. Because of their relative inaccessibility,
   they have not been included in the present study.

5. As of XXX/1 (July 1969) Dissertation Abstracts became
   Dissertation Abstracts International to reflect the
   projected enlargement of University Microfilms' dissertation publication program by the addition of dissertations from European universities.

Chapter 1

GENERAL BACKGROUND

A. General Definitions, Descriptions,
    Historical Background

The purpose of the works listed in this section is to
direct the reader to sources of definitions and descriptions
of rhythm. An attempt to cite them all would extend far
beyond the scope of the present work. Articles in music
dictionaries and encyclopedias which deal with rhythm or
related terms such as accent, beat, meter, period, tempo,
and time are excluded. For a practical introduction to
these sources, see the general article "Time" and its six
subsections by A. H. Fox-Strangways in Grove's Dictionary
of Music and Musicians (5th edition); "Rhythm" by Sir
Donald Francis Tovey in the Encyclopaedia Britannica (1951),
(also published in book form as Musical Articles from the
Encyclopaedia Britannica [London: Oxford University Press,
1944]); and "Accent" (1), "Meter, " "Rhythm, " and related
articles by Grosvenor Cooper in Harvard Dictionary of
Music (2nd edition, revised and enlarged; Cambridge, MA:
Belknap Press of Harvard University Press, 1969).

Also included in this section are generalized historical
studies, the most comprehensive of which is Curt Sachs's
Rhythm and Tempo: A Study in Music History (No. 24).

15

Specialized studies dealing with rhythm as used in particular geographical areas, periods of music history, and composers' styles are not included. Exceptions are the writings
of Carter (No. 3), Copland (No. 5), Eschman (No. 8), Fennell (No. 9), Kenyon (No. 16), and Wylie (No. 28) which
deal with rhythm in 20th-century or American music. A
list of specialized materials on rhythm and tempo performance practices between 1100 and 1900 may be found in
Performance Practice: A Bibliography, edited by Mary
Vinquist and Neal Zaslaw (New York: W. W. Norton & Co.,
Inc., 1971).

         See also B. Theory and Analysis (Nos. 29-52).

1. Barris, Chester. "Rhythm Puts Life into Music."
        Etude, LXVII/6 (June 1949) 340.
        A brief, general discussion of rhythm in piano per-
formance.

2. Borwick, Leonard. "Rhythm as Proportion." Music
        and Letters, VI/1 (Jan. 1925) 11-18.
        "Rhythm ... can come to being only if time-values
are absolute and time-elements strictly related and propor-
tioned."--p. 13. Examples from the music of Bach, Mozart, Beethoven, and Brahms are used to illustrate common
errors in the performance of rhythm.

3. Carter, Elliott. "The Rhythmic Basis of American
        Music." The Score, No. 12 (June 1955) 27-32.
        Investigates the influence of jazz rhythms on Ameri-
can music. Discusses the rhythmic innovations of Roy
Harris, Aaron Copland, Roger Sessions, Charles Ives,
Conlon Nancarrow, and Henry Brant.

4. Chanler, Theodore. "Rhythm and Habit." Modern
        Music, XXI/4 (May-June 1944) 208-11.
        Despairs of the tyranny of the regular pulse in con-
ventional music since it is habit forming and thus unstimu-
lating.

5. Copland, Aaron. "Jazz Structure and Influence."

Modern Music, IV/2 (Jan.-Feb. 1927) 9-14.
Surveys the rhythmic characteristics of jazz and describes their influence on "non-commercial" composers.
Forecasts an increased use of polyrhythm in American sym-
phonic music.

6. Cowell, Henry. "New Terms for New Music." Modern
    Music, V/4 (May-June 1928) 21-27.
Discusses the confusing definitions of "cross-rhythm,"
"poly-rhythm," and "counter-rhythm," and comments on Copland's use of the term "poly-rhythms" in his article, "Jazz
Structure and Influence" (see No. 5). Suggests and illustrates
a new system of terminology.

7. Dunk, John L. The Origin and Structure of Rhythm.
    London: James Clarke & Co., Ltd., 1952, 96 p.
A discussion couched in pseudo-scientific language of
the nature of rhythm as it is found in the arts and as it is
practiced. Includes definitions of rhythm from twenty-three
books and dictionaries. Covers topics such as "metaesthetic
units," "telesynthesis," and "hyperacoustics."
Truscott distills the book's thesis into two facts:
    ... (a) that lyrical tunes usually have a four-or eight-
    bar phrase structure, but that some composers ...
    write five, six or other irregular lengths. Mr. Dunk
    is not happy with this, and would prefer to see them
    lopped to a square four, since for him they are a four
    plus imposed extensions; (b) that rhythm which is
    complete in one bar and is simply repeated exact from
    bar to bar achieves no climax.
Review by Harold Truscott in Tempo, No. 28 (Summer
1953) 31-32.

8. Eschman, Karl H. Changing Forms in Modern Music.
    Boston: E. C. Schirmer Music Co., 1945. 180 p.
Chapter V, "The Measure of the Rhythm," discusses
rhythmic units and motives, accent, meter signatures, and
measure length in 20th-century music.

9. Fennell, Dorothy C. "Contemporary Rhythmic Devices."
    Unpublished M.M. thesis, Eastman School of Music,
    University of Rochester, 1939, 131 p.
An examination of some rhythmic devices used in 20th-
century music with the purpose of showing that rhythm is the
dominating feature of contemporary composition. Discusses
the following devices which were developed, according to the
author, for the attainment of rhythmic freedom and variety:
changing meter signatures, polymeter, polyrhythm, and "odd"

uses of rhythm such as $\frac{4+2+3}{8}$ meter, the isolated measure, and extremely long measures such as $\frac{19}{8}$. Contains 147 musical examples.

10. Gatty, Reginald. "Syncopation and Emphasis." Musical
     Times, LIII/832 (June 1912) 369-72; LIII/833 (July
     1912) 442-46.
        Attempts "... to co-ordinate the various scattered ex-
     planations with regard to syncopation and emphasis, and to
     reconcile the discrepancies that exist between them." Also
     shows "... that although vagueness of definition is partly re-
     sponsible for the confusion, there also prevails a widespread
     misconception as to the very nature of some of the effects in
     question."--p. 369.
        Forty musical examples from the classic and romantic
     periods are cited, and six types of syncopation are discussed.

11. Goetschius, Percy. "The Structure of Music: The Vital
     Functions of Rhythm in Music." Etude LI/3 (Mar.
     1933) 157-58.
        A general discussion of rhythm in music supported
     by twelve musical examples. Topics covered include Divi-
     sions of Time, The Beat, The Measure, Duple and Triple
     Meter, Compound Measures, Accentuation, Cross-Rhythms,
     Dual Rhythms, Other Unusual Rhythms, Irregular Measures,
     and The Ragged Rhythm. Although somewhat dated, the text
     is carefully organized and well repays reading.
        The article is reprinted as Chapter VII in the author's
     The Structure of Music: A Series of Articles Demonstrating
     in an Accurate, though Popular Manner, the Origin and Em-
     ployment of the Fundamental Factors of Music Structure and
     Composition ... (Philadelphia: Theodore Presser Co., 1934,
     170 p.).

12. Gow, George C. "Rhythm: The Life of Music." Mu-
     sical Quarterly, I/4 (Oct. 1915) 637-52.
        A general discussion, supported with numerous mu-
     sical examples, of the different manifestations rhythm may
     take in music. A partial listing of subtitles includes: Rhythm
     and Noise; Rhythm and Tone; Basis of Musical Rhythm;
     Lack of Adequate Notation; Volume, Length, Pitch and Figure
     Accent; Double Rhythms; Rhythms and Syncopation; Inter-
     polated Rhythms; and Rhythm and Form.

13. Granacher, Karl. "The Nature of Rhythm." Translated
     by Gertrude Bamberger. Music Educators Journal,
     L/4 (Feb.-Mar. 1964) 81-82.

Briefly discusses the use of silence in music and rhythm.

14.   Harris, Roy.   "Will We Produce a Second Rhythmic
         'Ars Nova'?"   Musical America, LIV/7 (Apr. 1934)
         14, 45.
         Traces the development of rhythm from "... Gre-
gorian chant to today's radicalism." Notes the current trend
for performing musicians to think of rhythms in their smallest
denominations rather than in their largest.

15.   Hawke, H. William.   "Rhythm in Performance."   Amer-
         ican Organist, XLI/9 (Sept. 1958) 327-31; XLI/10
         (Nov. 1958) 423-27.
         The first part of this two part article reviews defini-
tions of rhythm by Curt Sachs, Gustav Reese, and Henry
Cowell, and discusses pulse, meter, and rhythm as they relate to phrase length and total musical structure.
         The second part describes rhythmic performance on
the organ and explores the rhythms in the Eight Short Preludes and Fugues of J. S. Bach.

16.   Kenyon, Max.   "Modern Meters."   Music and Letters,
         XXVIII/2 (Apr. 1947) 168-74.
         States that complex, modern rhythms and meters are
often perceived as being simple and therefore should be treated
with suspicion.   Comments on the use of rhythm and meter in
the music of Mozart, Beethoven, and Bartók.

17.   Kirkpatrick, John.   "Metre and Rhythm in Performance."
         R. C. M. [Royal College of Music] Magazine, LXIII/2
         (1967) 46-48.   Reprinted from Cornell University Mu-
         sic Review, IX (1966).
         Discusses tempo rubato and the relation of additive
and divisive rhythms to meter.

18.   Krehbiel, James W.   "Rhythm, Meter and Syncopation."
         Unpublished M. M. thesis, Indiana University, 1958,
         79 p.
         Investigates the difference between rhythm and meter
(includes an historical survey and definitions), the psychological aspects of meter and rhythm, and the "principal object
of the thesis," syncopation.

19.   Kunst, Jaap.   Metre, Rhythm, Multi-Part Music.   Leiden:
         E. J. Brill, 1950, 47 p.
         Valuable for its etymological study of rhythmic

terminology. Defines and discusses meter, rhythm, duration,
arsis, thesis, poetic feet, polymeter, polyrhythm, tempo,
heterorhythm, polyphony, homophony, and heterophony using
forty-one musical examples of international origin, some of
which come from the author's own collection of Indonesian
folk music. (The author is the Curator of the Section of
Cultural Anthropology of the Royal Institute for the Indies in
Amsterdam.)

    Review by Frank Howes in Journal of the International
Folk Music Council, V (1953) 84.

20.   Lowe, C. Egerton. "What is Rhythm?" Musical Times,
       LXXXIII/1193 (July 1942) 202-3.

    Surveys definitions of rhythm from ten English ency-
clopedias and dictionaries of music.

21.   McEwen, Sir John B. The Thought in Music: An En-
       quiry into the Principles of Musical Rhythm, Phras-
       ing and Expression. London: Macmillan & Co.,
       Ltd., 1912, 233 p.

    Discusses rhythm, meter, tempo, accentuation,
rhythmic motive, rhythmic phrase, and rubato in relation to
the psychological basis of rhythm and the author's graphic
representation of rhythmical structure.

22.   Mathews, W. S. B. "The Nature of Musical Rhythm."
       Music, XXI/5 (Apr. 1902) 398-408.

    A discussion by the editor of Music. Offers defini-
tions of rhythm, time, bar, tempo, accent, motion, and
meter.

23.   Matthay, Tobias. Musical Interpretation: Its Laws and
       Principles, and Their Application in Teaching and
       Performing. London: Joseph Williams, Ltd., 1913,
       169 p. Reprinted by Greenwood Press, Westport,
       CT, 1970, 163 p.

    Intended primarily for pianists, but worth reading by
all musicians. Covers general principles of teaching and
learning; the nature of musical attention; the effect of time,
rhythm, and progression on musical shape; and tone-inflec-
tion, touch, fingering, and pedalling as applied to piano performance.

    Particularly valuable is the section describing two
types of rubato: the "leaning" type and the "push-on" type.
In both types the note durations in the phrase are altered
"... so as to enable us accurately to return to the pulse."--
p. 70.

        See McEwen's dissenting views in Tempo Rubato or
Time-Variation in Musical Performance (No. 89).

    Read, Gardner. Music Notation: A Manual of Modern
Practice. See No. 66.

24. Sachs, Curt. Rhythm and Tempo: A Study in Music
        History. New York: W. W. Norton & Co., Inc.,
        1953, 391 p.
        A musicological study which classifies rhythms as
divisive, additive, accentual, and numerical. Discusses types
of rhythms found in primitive tribes, in India, in the Near,
Middle, and Far East, and in ancient Israel, Greece, and
Rome. Examines the development of rhythm and tempo in
Western music. Two chapters are devoted to the Middle
Ages, two to the Renaissance, and one chapter each to the
Baroque, Rococo, Romantic, and the present.
        Of the eleven or more reviews available, the follow-
ing offer helpful criticism and corrections: Arnold Elston in
Journal of Aesthetics and Art Criticism, XII/2 (Dec. 1953)
276-77; Otto Gombosi in Journal of the American Musicological Society, VII/3 (Fall 1954) 221-28; Theodore F. Normann
in Journal of Research in Music Education, I/2 (Fall 1953)
143-45; Alexander L. Ringer in Musical Quarterly, XXXIX/2
(April 1953) 276-83; Charles Seeger in Notes, X/3 (June
1953) 435-38.

25. _____. "Rhythm and Tempo: An Introduction."
        Musical Quarterly, XXXVIII (July 1952) 384-98.
        Included almost verbatim as pp. 12-34 in the author's
Rhythm and Tempo: A Study in Music History (No. 24).

    Schafer, R. Murray. Ear Cleaning: Notes for an Ex-
perimental Music Course. See No. 249.

26. Straeten, E. van der. "Ear and Rhythm." Monthly
        Musical Record, XLVI/543 (Mar. 1916) 73-74;
        XLVI/544 (Apr. 1916) 106-7.
        Sketches concepts of rhythm from the ancient Greeks
to the present. Recommends using sounds heard in the en-
vironment to gain a feeling for rhythm.

27. Wolfe, Marian. "The Changing Time-Signature." Un-
        published M.M. thesis, Eastman School of Music,
        University of Rochester, 1939, 65 p.
        Traces the history of the "changing time-signature"
(multimeter) from its beginnings. Examines its use in music

of the 17th, 18th, and 19th centuries and the influences which
affected its use in serious compositions. Discusses the use
of quintuple meter, polymeter, and unusual or rare meter
signatures. Numerous musical examples are included.

28.   Wylie, Ruth S.   "Rhythm in Contemporary Music." Pro-
        ceedings of the Music Teachers National Association,
        XL (1946) 330-41.
        Examines the influence of ballet, jazz, incidental mu-
sic, folk music, and pre-classic rhythmic concepts on the
style of the modern composer. Examples of eight contemporary rhythmic devices are given. Recommendations are offered to educators, composers, music publishers, and general audiences for solutions to some of the rhythmic difficulties discussed.

B.   Theory and Analysis

        The materials in this section are of three types:
writings of an analytical nature such as Bie (No. 31), Biggs
(No. 32), Cooper and Meyer (No. 34), Creston (No. 37),
LaRue (No. 41), and Williams (No. 51); individualized rhythmic theories such as those of Cowell (No. 35), Glyn (No. 39),
Lussy (No. 42), and Schillinger (No. 48); and comprehensive
discussions of the rhythmic theories of other writers.   Of
this last type, the best chronological survey of rhythmic
theories from Aristoxenus to Schillinger is offered by Alette
(No. 29).   This may be supplemented by more specialized
studies such as those of Burton (No. 33) and Williams (Nos.
50 and 52).   Numerous theories written in languages other
than English have been excluded from a practical standpoint,
and since a great many of the most important of these have
already been covered in Carl Alette's dissertation (No. 29).

29.   Alette, Carl.   "Theories of Rhythm."   2 vols.   Unpub-
        lished Ph.D. dissertation, Eastman School of Music,
        University of Rochester, 1951, 323 p.
        "... presents in chronological order the ideas which

theorists from Aristoxenus to Schillinger have put forth concerning rhythm in music. In addition, it shows the general
stylistic characteristics of the use of rhythm in the actual music of each century. The over-all aim is to present a history
of the theory of rhythm in such a way as to contribute towards
the goal of a rhythmic theory for modern music."--Preface, p. ii.

30. Bernard, Edward. The Basic Principles of Rhythm in
    Music. Dorchester, MA: By the Author, 60 Ameri-
    can Legion Highway, 1968, 8 p.
       According to the author, "There are three basic
rhythmic principles in music, each of which establishes a
rhythmic pulse. These are: metrical rhythm, melodic
rhythm and harmonic rhythm."--p. 1. The principles are
discussed briefly, and suggestions are given for using them
in musical compositions.

31. Bie, Oscar. "Rhythm." Translated by Theodore Baker.
    Musical Quarterly, XI/4 (Oct. 1925) 331-38.
       A discussion of three aspects of rhythm: 1) rhythm
of a lower order, which includes a) a succession of equal
beats, b) dynamic rhythm, i.e., accented and unaccented
beats, and c) a combination of a and b; 2) rhythm of a
higher order, which pertains to the rhythmic organization of
an entire composition; and 3) the influence of popular dance
rhythms upon "serious" art music.
       Of interest is the discussion of a system of musical
metro-tectonics, i.e., the rhythmical grouping of the entire
"lay-out" of a composition, formulated by the Russian musical scientist, Professor Conus, and a comparison of this system with Hugo Riemann's theory of connecting melodic phrases.

32. Biggs, George B., Jr. "A Suggested Taxonomy of Mu-
    sic for Music Educators." Journal of Research in
    Music Education, XIX/2 (Summer 1971) 168-82.
       Classifies music into two basic areas: tone and time.
Each area is further divided into four levels, and these are arranged in the taxonomy according to their musical function. Includes explanations of terms used and their psychological implications, accompanied by references to four sources the author used
for information.

33. Burton, Martin C. "Changing Concepts of Rhythm in
    English Musical Writings, 1500-1740." Unpublished
    Ph.D. dissertation, Eastman School of Music, Uni-
    versity of Rochester, 1956, 386 p.
       A thorough investigation beginning with Renaissance

concepts of rhythm as found in Ornithoparcus' Micrologus
(1517) and concluding with James Grassineau's Dictionary of
Music (1740)--the first important musical dictionary in the
English language.

Chevé, Émile J. M.   The Theory of Music.   See No.
371.

34. Cooper, Grosvenor and Leonard B. Meyer.   The Rhyth-
        mic Structure of Music.   Chicago: University of
        Chicago Press, 1960, 212 p.
        An expansion of the analytic method proposed by
Meyer in Emotion and Meaning in Music (No. 102), pp. 102-
27, which may be further traced to the metro-tectonics of the
Russian musical scientist, Professor Conus, described by
Oscar Bie in "Rhythm" (No. 31), pp. 334-35.
        The book is designed to be used in conjunction with
courses in harmony, counterpoint, interpretation, and analysis. Its main thesis is that musical form, properly appre-
hended, is a macrorhythm. It proceeds from a discussion
of rhythm on the more obvious lower architectonic levels
through more complex rhythmic structures to an examination
of the larger forms.   Considers rhythm in relation to meter,
mobility, tension, continuity, form, and development.   Describes rhythmic groupings in terms generally associated with
prosody.   Extended analyses are given of Chopin's Prelude in
E-flat, Op. 24 and Beethoven's Symphony No. 8, Op. 93,
First Movement.
        See also No. 49, Peter Westergaard, "Some Problems
in Rhythmic Theory and Analysis."
        Review by Wallace Berry in Notes, XX/1 (Winter
1962-63) 60-61; Ellis B. Kohs in Journal of Music Theory,
V/1 (Apr. 1961) 129-34; Hans Tischler in Journal of the
American Musicological Society, XVI/2 (Summer 1963) 270-
72.

35. Cowell, Henry.   New Musical Resources.   New York:
        Alfred A. Knopf, 1930, 144 p.
        Reprinted with preface and notes by J. Godwin.   New
York: Something Else Press, Inc., 1969, 177 p.
        Introduces a theory of "musical relativity" by showing
that rhythm and tone, previously thought to be separate en-
tities are related through overtone ratios.   Cowell states that
his ideas on this subject were first conceived in 1919.
        Part II is devoted to rhythm with chapter titles as
follows: "Time," "Metre," "Dynamics," "Form," "Metre
and Time Combinations," "Tempo," "Scales of Rhythm."

Discusses "... the relationship of rhythm to sound-vibration, and, through this relationship and the application of overtone ratios, the building of ordered systems of harmony and counterpoint in rhythm, which have an exact relationship to tonal harmony and counterpoint."--p. 46.

Proposes a proportionate notation system dividing the measure into 3, 5, 7, 9, 11, 13, and 15 parts using differently shaped note heads. "Metric harmony" and the use of "scales" of rhythms, meters, and tempos are discussed. Includes a four-page glossary of musical terms.

36.   Creston, Paul. "The Importance of Being Rhythmic."
       Instrumentalist, XVII/10 (June 1963) 30-32.
       A condensation of the major points in the author's
Principles of Rhythm (No. 37).

37.   _____. Principles of Rhythm. New York: Franco
       Colombo, Inc., 1961, 1964, 216 p.
       Designed as a practical text for students of composition, this book is also useful as a general instructional and analytical aid.

It deals with the mensurable rhythms of Western music from the 17th century to the present. Discussed are the elements of rhythm: meter, pace, accent, and pattern; pre-Classic dance rhythms; five basic rhythmic structures: regular subdivision, irregular subdivision, overlapping, regular subdivision overlapping, and irregular subdivision overlapping; polymeters and polyrhythms; compositional rubato: syncopation; basic rhythmic patterns; and rhythm structure as a whole. Appendix I outlines principal ancient Greek meters, rhythmic modes, medieval meters, and 16th-century meters. Solutions to the exercises found at the end of each chapter are contained in Appendix II. Contains a wealth of musical examples. Discussions of some subjects are scattered throughout the book, making the absence of an index an unfortunate omission.

Creston's Six Preludes, Op. 38 for piano (New York: Leeds Music Corp., 1949) were written as examples of the five rhythmic structures discussed in Principles of Rhythm.

See also Creston's letter to the Music Educators Journal LV/6 (Feb. 1969) 15-16.

38.   _____. "The Structure of Rhythm." Clavier, X/8
       (Nov. 1971) 15-23.
       An explanation and analysis of the rhythmic principles involved in the composer's Six Preludes, Op. 38 for piano (see No. 37). The music to Prelude No. 1 is included. Also

recounts the reasons which prompted Creston to write the
preludes and Principles of Rhythm.

    Fletcher, Grant. Rhythm--Notation and Production.
See No. 55.

39. Glyn, Margaret H. Analysis of the Evolution of Musical
      Form. London: Longmans, Green & Co. , 1909,
      331 p.
    Continues the theoretical discussion presented in
Rhythmic Conception of Music (No. 40). "The object of the
present volume [is] ... the application of the evolutionary
principle to practical music, the essential motive power of
which is to be found in rhythm."--Preface.
    Defines the nature of rhythm as the periodic quality
of all movement and classifies it into three types: the pulsa-
tive or beating rhythm, the circling or centering rhythm, and
the undulating or wave-rhythm. Discusses rhythm as the
underlying unity of musical form.
    See also Margaret H. Glyn, Theory of Musical Evo-
lution (London: J. M. Dent & Sons, Ltd. , 1934, 315 p.).

40. _____. Rhythmic Conception of Music. London:
      Longmans, Green & Co. , 1907, 191 p.

41. LaRue, Jan. Guidelines for Style Analysis. New York:
      W. W. Norton & Co. , Inc. , 1970, 244 p.
    Included for its scholarly, perceptive approach to
rhythmic analysis. Chapter V discusses rhythmic layers,
component states, and typology; rhythmic contributions to
shape; and rhythm in large, middle, and small dimensions.
    Review by Graham George in Notes, XXVIII/4 (June
1972) 680-81; Roland Jackson in Journal of the American
Musicological Society, XXIV/3 (Fall 1971) 489-92.

42. Lussy, Mathis. Musical Expression, Accents, Nuances,
      and Tempo, in Vocal and Instrumental Music. Trans-
      lated from the 4th ed. by M. E. von Glehn. London:
      Novello, Ewer & Co. , [1892], 236 p.
    "... offers an explanation of the causes and myster-
ious laws of expression; ... [and] rules as regards tempo,
accents, and nuances, ..."--Preface, p. iv.
    States that the "phenomena" of musical expression
consists of three types of accentuation: 1) metrical accent
which comes at the beginning of every measure (metrical accent appeals to the instinct); 2) rhythmical accent which dis-
tinguishes one rhythmic unit from another and may or may

not coincide with the metrical accent (rhythmical accent appeals to the intellect); and 3) expressive accent which be-
longs to those notes which tend to destroy the metrical and
rhythmical accent (expressive accent appeals to the senti-
ment). The main body of the book discusses and illustrates
the three types of accent.
　　　See also the discussion in Alette's "Theories of
Rhythm" (No. 29), pp. 203-23.

43. _____. A Short Treatise on Musical Rhythm.
　　　　　Abridged by E. Dutoit. Translated by Ernest
　　　　　Fowles. London: Vincent Music Co. , Ltd. , 1908,
　　　　　82 p.
　　　Translated from Le rythme musical, son origine, sa
fonction et son accentuation (Paris: Au Ménestrel, Heugel et
Cie. , 1883, 105 p.).

44. Murray, Edward and Howard L. Edsall. "An Unexplored
　　　　　Musical Resource. " Journal of the Franklin Institute,
　　　　　CCXXXVII/6 (June 1944) 451-467.
　　　According to the authors, the unexplored resource in
music is the writing of contrapuntal lines in different time
signatures, in ratios more extended than two against three,
or three against four.
　　　The authors state that these "Coincident meters are
merely syncopations and cross accents which, from being occasional and spasmodic, have been erected into a formal and
established musical structure. "--p. 453.
　　　Two limitations in using coincident meters are given:
1) they can be clearly expressed only where a variety of tone
color is available, as in an orchestra, chamber ensemble, or
organ; and 2) the conductor must be able to conduct both
meters simultaneously.

45. Pike, Alfred. "The Time Set as a Rhythmic Agent for
　　　　　the Series. " Music Review, XXIV/2 (May 1963)
　　　　　168-75.
　　　Discusses the derivation and application of a time
set through serial and non-serial procedures. Suggests ways
of computing various rhythmic contexts for the series.

　　　Sachs, Curt. Rhythm and Tempo: A Study in Music
History. See No. 24.

46. Schillinger, Joseph. Encyclopedia of Rhythms: Instru-
　　　　　mental Forms of Harmony, a Massive Collection of
　　　　　Rhythm Patterns (Evolved According to the Schillinger

Theory of Interference), Arranged in Instrumental
Form. New York: Charles Colin, 1966, 250 p.
    A handbook, consisting mostly of music written on
two staves, which presents many basic rhythms and their
interference patterns as derived from The Schillinger System
of Musical Composition (see No. 48). Includes "A Note to
the Teacher and Student" by Arnold Shaw which places
Schillinger's system in historical perspective, and a "Supplementary and Explanatory Key" by Charles Colin.

47. _____. The Mathematical Basis of the Arts. New
        York: Philosophical Library, 1948, 696 p.
        Review by Joseph Yasser in Notes, VI/3 (June 1949)
    465-68.

48. _____. The Schillinger System of Musical Composi-
        tion. 4th ed. 2 vols. New York: Carl Fischer,
        Inc. , 1946, 1640 p.
        Synthesizes music theory and the laws of physics,
psychology, and mathematics. Schillinger's theory of rhythm
is expounded in the first of the twelve books which comprise
these two volumes. Rhythm is the result of the interference
of two or more synchronized periodicities (equally-spaced im-
pulses).
                    In Schillinger's system, rhythm refers not only to
                what is ordinarily called rhythm, that is, the divi-
                sion of time within a single measure or small
                group of measures (Fractional Rhythm) [underlined
                words are set in bold face type in the original],
                but also to the way in which the measures them-
                selves are organized into groups (Factorial
                Rhythm). According to the fractional technique,
                a single duration of time of any length is sub-
                divided binomially (into two parts), trinomially
                (into three parts), or polynomially (into n parts)
                according to one or more Style-Series. The re-
                sults of this subdivision, or fractioning, are the
                rhythm. The results may be subjected to factorial
                technique, by which a group of durations is de-
                veloped into larger groups. Such results may be
                distributed in a number of ways over a number of
                simultaneous instrumental parts. Every aspect of
                music is, in Schillinger's system, controlled funda-
                mentally by his rhythmic techniques ... Schillinger
                does not restrict the concept of rhythm to time
                and the durations of attacks. He deals also with
                1). instrumental rhythm--the pattern according to

which instruments enter and leave an ensemble;
2). intonational rhythm--the pattern of pitches in
a phrase; and 3). harmonic rhythm--the pattern
of harmonic groups in a sequence. "--Glossary,
compiled by Lyle Dowling and Arnold Shaw,
p. 1622.
Review by Thomas Munro in Journal of Aesthetics
and Art Criticism, VIII/2 (Dec. 1949) 131-32.
See also Nos. 46 and 47.

49. Westergaard, Peter. "Some Problems in Rhythmic
Theory and Analysis." Perspectives of New Music,
I/1 (Fall 1962) 180-91.
Surveys the state of rhythmic theory and comments
on the chief attractions and failures of the analytic methods
of Cooper and Meyer in The Rhythmic Structure of Music
(No. 34).
Presents an analysis of the third movement of
Webern's Piano Variations, Op. 27 which demonstrates the
differential role of rhythm in creating pitch relationships,
and some ways in which pitch relationships create a sense
of rhythm, particularly large-scale rhythm.
See also further comment by Edward T. Cone and
William J. Mitchell in "Communications." Perspectives of
New Music, I/2 (Spring 1963) 206-11.

50. Williams, C. F. Abdy. The Aristoxenian Theory of
Musical Rhythm. Cambridge: University Press,
1911, 191 p.
One of the few books in English on the subject. Dis-
cusses and analyzes the rhythmic theory of Aristoxenus of
Tarentum and surveys the writings of Aristides Quintilianus,
Hephaestion, Baccheios the Elder, St. Augustine, and others.
Examines rhythmic practices in ancient Greek music and
their relation to rhythm in 18th- and 19th-century music.

51. _____. The Rhythm of Modern Music. London:
Macmillan & Co. , Ltd. , 1909, 321 p.
A general discussion of sixty-five aspects of rhythm,
including phrasing, accentuation, meter, and tempo. Analyzes
rhythmic structure in the music of Beethoven, Brahms,
Chopin, Debussy, D'Indy, Dvorák, Elgar, Grieg, Haydn,
Kuhac, Mozart, Schumann, Stanford, R. Strauss, and Tchai-
kovsky. A seven-page explanation of Hugo Riemann's theory
of agogic accent is appended.

52. _____. "Some Ancient Conceptions of Rhythm. "

Musical Times, LXIV/960 (Feb. 1923) 105-6.
Cites some affective qualities of ancient Greek
rhythmical forms.

C.   Notation

Since accurate and artistic performance, effective
teaching, and thorough understanding of rhythm depend to a
large extent on the comprehension of its notation, a separate
section has been devoted to this aspect.   The literature includes
discussions on the notation of modern rhythm by Copland (No.
53), Karkoschka (No. 55b), Perkins (No. 65), and Stone (No.
69); experimental research on rhythmic notation by Gregory
(No. 55a), Linger (No. 56), Macferran (No. 58), Minaglia (No.
60), Mortenson (No. 62), Osborn (No. 63), Peitersen (No. 64),
Rohner (No. 68), and Wheelwright (No. 70); and particularly
useful general guides to traditional and modern usage and notation such as those by Fletcher (No. 55) and Read (No. 66).

Musicological studies concerned with notes inégales,
figura corta, ornamentation, and other rhythmic interpreta-
tional practices are not covered here.   For a bibliography of
these writings see Thurston Dart, The Interpretation of Music
(London: Hutchison & Co., 1954);   Robert Donington, The
Interpretation of Early Music (2nd ed.; New York: St. Mar-
tin's Press, 1965);   Robert M. Haas, Aufführungspraxis der
Musik (Wildpark-Potsdam: Akademische Verlagsgesellschaft
Athenaion, 1931);   and Mary Vinquist and Neal Zaslaw (eds.),
Performance Practice: A Bibliography (New York: W. W.
Norton & Co., Inc., 1971).

53.   Copland, Aaron.   "On the Notation of Rhythm."   Modern
         Music, XXI/4 (May-June 1944) 217-20.
         Discusses the tyranny of the bar line in 20th-century
music.   Recommends writing rhythmic units of two's and

three's so that they look the way they sound.

     Cowell, Henry. <u>New Musical Resources</u>. See No. 35.

54. Crowder, Louis. "Notation: Is Rhythm Really Becoming More Complex? Or Is the Notation Merely More Accurate?" <u>Clavier</u>, IV/4 (Sept. 1965) 24-31.
     A perceptive, analytical survey of unorthodox rhythmic notation found in the piano works of Bach, Chopin, Schumann, Schubert, Debussy, and Ravel.

55. Fletcher, Grant. <u>Rhythm--Notation and Production.</u>
Tempe, AZ: By the Author, 1626 E. Williams St., 1969, 178 p.
     A scholarly consideration of rhythmic notational and performance problems illustrated by numerous musical examples. Historical, interpretative, and psychological aspects of rhythm are included. Discusses the effect of non-rhythmic elements upon rhythmic stress perception, and the effect of duration, metric pulsation, and dynamic accent upon styles of composition and styles of performance.
     The appendix contains useful charts illustrating fractional divisions of dotted notes and "plain" (undotted) notes and a list of rhythmic notational abbreviations.

     Gordon, Edwin. <u>The Psychology of Music Teaching</u>.
See No. 98.

55a. Gregory, Thomas B. "The Effect of Rhythmic Notation Variables on Sight-Reading Errors." <u>Journal of Research in Music Education</u>, XX/4 (Winter 1972) 462-68.
     Based on the author's master's thesis, "An Analysis of the Effect of Various Types of Rhythmic Notation on the Errors Made in Music Sight-Reading" (Kent State University, 1967).
              The study sought to identify error differences resulting from four different representations of rhythmic stimuli: in notation spaced conventionally in regard to rhythm, notation spaced conventionally in regard to rhythm but with the beats indicated, notation spaced in proportion to its rhythmic duration [see No. 70, Lorin F. Wheelwright, <u>An Experimental Study of the Perceptibility and Spacing of Music Symbols</u>], and notation incorporating stemless note heads elongated in proportion to the

notes' durations [see No. 63, Leslie A. Osborn,
"Notation Should Be Metric and Representational"].
--p. 463.

Subjects were B^b soprano clarinetists drawn from
grades seven through twelve. The two null hypotheses for
the study were accepted: "... that the total number of errors
made in an instrumental sight-reading performance is not affected significantly by the spatial logic of the rhythmic factor
in the notation." and "... that the number of rhythmic errors
made in an instrumental sight-reading performance is not affected significantly by the spatial logic of the rhythmic factor
in the notation."--p. 462.

    Jenkins, Harry. "Teaching Syncopation." See No.
381.

55b. Karkoschka, Erhard. Notation in New Music: A Criti-
    cal Guide to Interpretation and Realisation. Trans-
    lated by Ruth Koenig. New York: Praeger Pub-
    lishers, Inc., 1972, 183 p. Originally entitled Das
    Schriftbild der Neuen Musik (Celle: Hermann Moeck
    Verlag, 1966, 185 p. and 3 charts).
        Notation in New Music provides music-teachers,
        composers, and performers with an analysis of
        several types of new notations, as well as with
        the elements of a musical vocabulary capable of
        expressing contemporary ideas. It sets the cate-
        gories and phenomena of new notation in syste-
        matic order and makes proposals for common use.
            The opening chapter of the book surveys the
        most important present-day phenomena in notation
        and discusses the criteria for evaluating them.
        There follows a chapter on tempered notation, in
        which the author shows that absolutely precise
        and complicated rhythms can be better expressed
        and more clearly notated by means of distances
        than by traditional symbols and discusses ...
        [eight] requirements that new notation must fulfill
        in order to be efficient for the present--and, as
        far as can be foreseen, for the future. After a
        brief reference to the various reforms that have
        been suggested, he enters into a detailed discus-
        sion of Klavarscribo and Equitone, 'the only two
        experimental forms of the past and present worthy
        of discussion.' Extensive coverage is given to
        Equitone, which the author favors; ... Next come
        chapters devoted to exact notation, frame notation,

indicative notation, ... musical graphics [and the
notation of electronic music]. In each chapter,
the symbols are arranged according to their basic
aspects, such as tempo, meter, duration, and
pitch, and according to the musicians for whose
use they are intended--general symbols applying
to various instruments, symbols for conductors,
keyboard instruments, and so forth. The final
chapter is devoted to a ... collection of [eighty-
nine] notational examples [almost entirely by
European composers] with explanations."--jacket
notes.
    Included are over seventy-three tempo, meter, and
duration symbols used in exact, frame, and indicative notation. Unfortunately,
        ... Karkoschka fails to provide a comprehensive
        catalogue and analysis of proposals and systems
        dealing with an extension or reorganization of the
        arsenal of traditional durational symbols. ...
        He does not even mention proposals such as that
        by Henry Cowell.... --pp. 151-52 of review by
        Kurt Stone in Perspectives of New Music, V/2
        (Spring-Summer 1967) 146-54.
    See also review by Roger Smalley in Music and
Musicians, XXI/4 (Dec. 1972) 22-25.

56. Linger, Bernard L.   An Experimental Study of Dura-
        tional Notation.   Ph.D. dissertation, Florida State
        University, 1966, 113 p. ;   LC 66-9071;   DA
        XXVII/4A, 1073.
    Investigates accuracy in the performance of conven-
tionally-notated durational patterns as affected by perceptual
differences among college students who were non-music majors. Regarding notational symbols as an indirect indication
of duration resulted in a significantly more accurate performance and more consistent choice of tempo than thinking of
the symbols as a direct indication.

57. McEwen, John B.   "Rhythm and Phrasing: Some Mis-
        conceptions."   Monthly Musical Record, XLVIII/570
        (June 1918) 126-28.
    Comments on the semantic meanings of the two terms.
Proposes a method of indicating the rhythmic "outline" in music by using the bar line only before the "accented nucleus"
of each unit.

58. Macferran, Marilyn E.   "The Optimum Spacing of

Music Symbols for Rhythmic Perception." Unpublished M. S. thesis, University of Kansas, 1947,
100 p.
Based on Wheelwright's research (see No. 70). Discusses vertical and horizontal inter-note distance, Wheelwright's time-space ratio, use of flags and beams, and bar
line placement.

59.   Mansfield, Orlando A.   "The Dot and the Double Dot."
Etude, XXXII/1 (Jan. 1914) 19-20.
Sketches the history of the dot in musical notation
from the end of the fourth century A. D.   Discusses the durational values of the double and triple dot, and the use of the
dot in expressing staccato, tenuto, fermatas, tremolo, and
measure repetitions.

60.   Minaglia, Don E.   "A Controlled Experiment in Rhythm
Instruction and in Learning the Letter Names of
Notes for Fourth Grade Students Utilizing 'Musica'
a Proposed Music Notation."   Unpublished M. M. thesis, Northwestern University, 1960, 178 p.
A study comparing learning conventional notation with
learning Mūsica, a notation invented by Traugott Rohner (see
No. 68).   Results of the rhythm reading test indicate no statistically significant difference between learning the two nota-
tions.   However, letter names of notes were more readily
and correctly learned using Mūsica.

61.   Moore, Aubrey.   "Improving Meter Notation."   Instrumentalist, XXII/4 (Nov. 1967) 39.
Suggests eliminating the bottom number in meter
signatures and substituting a note-symbol for the unit or beat.

62.   Mortenson, Glenn R.   Development and Use of Com-
puterized Procedures for Scoring Sight Reading of
Rhythms to Compare the Effectiveness of Metric and
Representational Notation with Conventional Notation.
Ph. D. dissertation, Northwestern University, 1970,
197 p. ; LC 71-1924.
Based on Osborn's research (see No. 63).   Evaluates
metric-representational and traditional notation in regard to
their effect on the ability to sight read rhythms after a period
of training.   Constructs objective procedures for evaluating
rhythmic performance and assesses student acceptance of the
rhythm training and metric-representational notation.

63.   Osborn, Leslie A.   "Notation Should be Metric and

Representational." Journal of Research in Music
Education, XIV/2 (Summer 1966) 67-83.
Investigates the following features of metric-representational notation: equidistant spacing of bar lines; equidistant representation of the pulse within the measure, identified by a short interruption of the inner three lines of the
staff; proportionate linear spacing of note values; and representation of note duration by horizontal length of the note
heads.
See also No. 55a, Thomas B. Gregory, "The Effect
of Rhythmic Notation Variables on Sight-Reading Errors."

64. Peitersen, Dana N. An Experimental Evaluation of the
     Transfer Effects of Rhythm Training in Spaced Nota-
     tion on Subsequent Reading of Commercially Printed
     Music. Ph. D. dissertation, University of Minnesota,
     1954, 312 p.; LC A54-1443; DA XIV/6, 983-84.
     Compares the rhythmic performances of two groups
of junior high school instrumentalists after they received
rhythmic training which differed with regard to the time-
space ratio of note values. The advantages of spaced notation appear to be confined to the immediate reading of music
so prepared.

65. Perkins, John M. "Note Values." Perspectives of
     New Music, III/2 (Spring-Summer 1965) 47-57.
     Offers analog notation as a simple and direct method
of expressing unlimited numbers of "irrational" durational relationships. Provides insight to the music of the Darmstadt
composers and Elliott Carter.

66. Read, Gardner. Music Notation: A Manual of Modern
     Practice. 2nd ed. Boston: Allyn and Bacon, Inc.,
     1969, 482 p.
     Contains a brief history of music notation and sec-
tions on the elements of notation, idiomatic notation, and
manuscript technique. Included in the present study for its
unique and valuable discussion of traditional and modern usage
and notation of meter and rhythm. Furnishes tables of meter
signatures, compound meters, fractional meters, and unequal
note-groups. Examines unusual meter signatures, alternating
meters, variable meters, combined meters, compound meters,
polymeters, mixed meters, fractional meters, decimal meters,
conducting patterns, dotted bar lines as employed to depict
inner subdivisions of complex rhythms or to show the structure of compound meters, and the notation of irregular note-
groups.

Review of 1st ed. by Paul A. Pisk in <u>Notes</u>, XXII/3
(Spring 1966) 1039. Review of 2nd ed. by Peter J. Pirie in
<u>Music Review</u>, XXXI/2 (May 1970) 169-70; Tim Souster in
<u>Tempo</u>, No. 89 (Summer 1969) 34-35.

67. _____. "Some Problems of Rhythmic Notation."
        <u>Journal of Music Theory</u>, IX/1 (Spring 1965) 153-62.
        A compact, perceptive discussion of three methods
of notating unequal groups, i.e., triplets against duplets or
quadruplets, quintuplets against triplets, etc. The relative
prevalence of the three methods was determined by an examination of 200 works chosen at random from the late 19th
and the 20th centuries. The practice of writing double figures
for unequal note-groups, i.e., $\frac{3}{8}$ ♫♫♫ is treated briefly.

Serves as excellent background material for Chapter XI,
"Barlines and Rhythm," in Read's <u>Music Notation: A Manual
of Modern Practice</u>, 2nd ed. (No. 66).

68. Rohner, Traugott. <u>Mūsica: An Improved Modern Sys-
        tem of Music Notation</u>. Evanston, IL: Instrumen-
        talist Co., 1968, 12 p.
        Describes Mūsica, a notation devised by the author
which uses a six-line staff. New rhythmic aspects of Mūsica
include proportional spacing of notes and rests, the use of
diamond-shaped note heads for triplet subdivisions of the beat,
new symbols for rests, and new terminology for the durational value of notes.
        See also No. 60, Don E. Minaglia, "A Controlled
Experiment in Rhythm Instruction...."

69. Stone, Kurt. "Problems and Methods of Notation."
        <u>Perspectives of New Music</u>, I/2 (Spring 1963) 9-31.
        An excellent survey of contemporary systems of no-
tating pitch, tempo, rhythm, meter, and articulation. Contains numerous musical illustrations. Limited to a discussion
of published works or works about to be published. Henry
Cowell's proportionate notation system using differently shaped
note heads is explained and placed in historical perspective
(see No. 35). Practical disadvantages of proportionate notation are discussed and some compromises are suggested.

        Tenaglia, Richard. "Teaching Counting with the New
Math." See No. 403.

        Van Patten, Leroy. <u>Revised Standard Notation of TIME
in Music</u>. See No. 268.

70.   Wheelwright, Lorin F.   An Experimental Study of the
       Perceptibility and Spacing of Music Symbols.   Ph. D.
       dissertation.   New York: Bureau of Publications,
       Teachers College, Columbia University, 1939, 116 p.
       Conclusions which pertain to rhythm indicate that:
          1.   Spacing is not used consistently or precisely
          in children's song materials to indicate time
          values.
          2.   Patterns of notes are successively compared
          more accurately when spaced in consistent propor-
          tion to time values than when not so spaced.
          3.   Music is sight-read and performed at the
          piano with significantly fewer errors when the
          symbols are spaced in proportion to their time
          values than when spaced in the traditional man-
          ner. --p. 3.
       See also No. 55a, Thomas B. Gregory, "The Effect
of Rhythmic Notation Variables on Sight-Reading Errors" and
No. 58, Marilyn E. Macferran, "The Optimum Spacing of
Music Symbols for Rhythmic Perception. "

71.   Wood, Ralph W.   "The Rickety Bar. "   Musical Times,
       XCV/1338 (Aug. 1954) 412-15.
       Discusses the use of meter and bar line especially
in the works of Stravinsky.

D.   Tempo

       Over one-third of the items listed here are concerned
with the performance of tempo rubato; Aronowsky (No. 73)
and Reddick (No. 92) provide performance times of numerous
works, thus enabling conductors, vocalists, and instrumentalists to make a fair estimate of proper tempi for performance; and Franz (No. 81), Harding (No. 84), and Wilson
(No. 94) treat the history and usage of the metronome.

       For the most part, literature on historical and
stylistic aspects of tempo is not covered in the present study.

       See also Chapter 2, D.   Perception of Tempo
(Nos. 183-187).

72.   Anderson, Alice J.   "A Study of Tempo Rubato." Un-
        published M. M. thesis, Eastman School of Music,
        University of Rochester, 1948, 89 p.
        Discusses various aspects and definitions of rubato,
traces its historical development, and indicates, especially
to the pianist, how it is used in current performance.

73.   Aronowsky, S [olomon]. Performing Times of Orches-
        tral Works.   London: Ernest Benn, Ltd. , 1959,
        802 p.
        A comprehensive work; gives timings for individual
movements as well as for complete works.   Pages xiii-xxix
provide addresses of music publishers' organizations, music
publishers, and performing rights and collecting societies.
Excessively large type and wide spacing and margins make
the book unwieldy and expensive.

74.   Brower, Harriette.   "The Marriage of Rhythm and
        Rubato. " Etude, XLIV/11 (Nov. 1926) 805-6.
        Deals with the use of rubato in piano music, espe-
cially that of Chopin.   Cites four ways rubato may be performed, and states that true artistic rubato occurs when the
left hand plays in strict tempo while the right hand hurries
or retards slightly.

75.   Cauchie, Maurice.   "Respect for Rhythm. "   Translated
        by Fred Rothwell.   Musical Courier, CII/9 (May 9,
        1931) 6.
            Respect for the rhythm of a piece of music means
            being exact as regards the general pace at which
            it is to be taken, carefully setting forth the var-
            ious rhythmical figures, and seeing that these
            figures are not misrepresented in the rallentando
            and accelerando passages. --p. 6.
        This article, with a modified title, is a chapter in
the author's book, Cours d'Education musicale à l'usage des
instrumentistes, chanteurs, organisateurs de concerts, et
chefs d'orchestre de tout age.

76.   Christensen, Dieter.   "Inner Tempo and Melodic Tempo. "
        Translated by Bruno Nettl.   Ethnomusicology, IV/1
        (Jan. 1960) 9-14.
        Presents a different approach to solving the problems
discussed by Kolinski in "The Evaluation of Tempo" (No. 86).
        See also No. 87, Mieczyslaw Kolinski, "Notes on
Christensen's Article: 'Inner Tempo and Melodic Tempo. ' "

Cort, Henry R., Jr. Tempo and Expressive Properties of Auditory Figures: A Psychophysical Study. See
No. 183.

77. Culshaw, John. "Tempo Mannerisms." Chesterian,
XXVII/172 (Oct. 1952) 44-46.
Decries the overuse of rubato in the performance of
classical and romantic orchestral repertory.

Farnsworth, Paul R.; Harold A. Block; and Ward
C. Waterman. "Absolute Tempo." See No. 184.

78. Fielden, Thomas. "Tempo Rubato." Music and
Letters, XXXIV/2 (Apr. 1953) 150-52.
Notes that the interpretation of tempo rubato in the
piano works of Chopin too often degenerates into mere dis-
tortion. Also discusses the use of rubato in the works of
Bach, Beethoven, and Brahms. Cites four rules for performing rubato.

79. Finck, Henry T. Success in Music, and How It Is Won.
New York: Charles Scribner's Sons, 1909, 471 p.
Chapter XXVIII, "[Ignace Jan] Paderewski on Tempo
Rubato," presents a brief, masterful study of the technique
and interpretation of rubato, especially as related to 19th-
century piano music.

80. Frampton, John R. "Some Evidence for the Natural-
ness of the Less Usual Rhythms." Musical Quarterly,
XII/3 (July 1926) 400-405.
Contains analyses of selected sections of recorded
performances of piano works by Chopin, Grieg, and Liszt.
Individual artistic interpretations employing rubato are notated to show that they were performed in "artificial" "quintuple," "septuple," and "nonuple" rhythm.

81. Franz, Frederick. Metronome Techniques: Being a
Very Brief Account of the History and Use of the
Metronome with Many Practical Applications for the
Musician. New Haven, CT: Yale University Press,
1947, 52 p.
An attempt to supply knowledge of the subtle use of
metronome technique "... to acquire concert-performance-
control of rhythm with all its nuances."--Prelude.
Includes many unusual and practical hints on using
the metronome as a tempo standard and for acquiring rhythmic skill. Contains a short, rather unscholarly history of
the metronome.

82.   Gatty, Reginald. "Tempo Rubato." Musical Times,
         LIII/829 (Mar. 1912) 160-62.
      Traces the history and discusses four different uses
of tempo rubato.

83.   Gehrkens, Karl W. "Rhythm in Music." Music Edu-
         cators Journal, XLIX/5 (Apr.-May 1963) 45-46.
      Comments on rhythmical flexibility and artistic taste
in musical performance.

84.   Harding, Rosamond E. M. Origins of Musical Time
         and Expression. London: Oxford University Press,
         1938, 115 p.
      Contains four unusual musicological studies. It is
included here for the first of these, entitled "The Metronome
and Its Precursors" (pp. 1-35). The precursors are discussed chronologically, beginning with the influence and writings of the Italian astronomer and physicist Galileo and the
monk Zacconi in the 16th and 17th centuries; continuing with
the devices of such men as Mersenne, Loulié, Affillard,
Tans'ur, Wright, and Smart in the 17th and 18th centuries;
and concluding with the inventions of Winkel and Mälzel in
the early 19th century. Includes illustrations and the text
of primary sources describing many of the devices. Also
relates Beethoven's influence on the acceptance of Mälzel's
metronome. Appendixes offered are: "I. A Suggestion that
Clementi Be Asked To Fix the Metronome Tempi," "II. Hec-
tor Berlioz on an Electric Metronome by van Bruge," and
"III. Bibliography" of fifty items including original patents,
instructions on the performance of tempo found in early tutors, and other writings relating to the metronome.

      Hodgson, Walter. "Absolute Tempo: Its Existence,
Extent, and Possible Explanation." See No. 186.

85.   Johnstone, J. Alfred. Rubato, or the Secret of Ex-
         pression in Pianoforte Playing. London: Joseph
         Williams, Ltd. , 1920, 56 p.
      A comprehensive study of rubato. Contains discus-
sions and analyses of rhythmic, motive, phrasing, and tempo
variations in examples from the keyboard music of Bach,
Mozart, Beethoven, Mendelssohn, and Chopin. Gives views
on rubato by eminent artists, composers, and musicologists.

      Kirkpatrick, John. "Metre and Rhythm in Performance."
See No. 17.

86. Kolinski, Mieczyslaw. "The Evaluation of Tempo."
      Ethnomusicology, III/2 (May 1959) 45-57.
      States that songs analyzed in the field of ethnomu-
sicology which have similar metronomic indications often dif-
fer widely in the kind and frequency of the durational values
employed, implying a considerable contrast in their actual
tempo. Suggests that the speed of each piece should be expressed by a figure that indicates the average lapse of time
between two consecutive notes, i.e., the average number of
consecutive notes contained within a specified time unit, such
as one minute.
      See also No. 76, Dieter Christensen, "Inner Tempo
and Melodic Tempo"; and No. 87, Mieczyslaw Kolinski,
"Notes on Christensen's Article:...."

87. _____. "Notes on Christensen's Article: 'Inner
      Tempo and Melodic Tempo.'" Ethnomusicology,
      IV/1 (Jan. 1960) 14-15.
      Contains further comments on Kolinski's own
article "The Evaluation of Tempo" (No. 86), and refutations
on Christensen's article, "Inner Tempo and Melodic Tempo"
(No. 76).

88. Laycock, Ralph G. "Flexibility of Tempo." Instru-
      mentalist, XXV/2 (Sept. 1970) 86; XXV/4 (Nov.
      1970) 64-66, XXV/5 (Dec. 1970) 57-59.
      A comprehensive treatment designed for the instru-
mentalist and conductor. Discusses solutions to problems
arising from varying tempi in order to achieve artistic performance. Suggests techniques for effective rehearsal of
such passages.

      Lund, Max W. "An Analysis of the 'True Beat' in
Music." See No. 187.

      Lussy, Mathis. Musical Expression, Accents, Nuances
and Tempo, in Vocal and Instrumental Music. See No.
42.

89. McEwen, Sir John B. Tempo Rubato or Time-Variation
      in Musical Performance. London: Oxford University
      Press, 1928, 47 p.
      Demonstrates by means of a critical examination of
performances by great pianists recorded on piano rolls
(known as "Duo-Art" rolls, published by the Aeolian Co.,
London) that the rules concerning rubato, as stated by
writers such as Tobias Matthay in Musical Interpretation:

... (see No. 23) and the author himself in <u>The Thought in
Music: ...</u> (See No. 21) have no real validity. An appendix
contains a discussion of the definition of rubato, the sense of
time, the continuity of tempo, and the attentive process.

 Matthay, Tobias. <u>Musical Interpretation: Its Laws
and Principles, and Their Application in Teaching and Per-
forming</u>. See No. 23.

90. Niecks, Frederick. "Tempo Rubato." <u>Monthly Musical
   Record</u>, XLIII/506 (Feb. 1913) 29-31; XLIII/507
   (Mar. 1913) 58-59.
   Defines the meaning of tempo rubato and surveys its
use in the music and writings of Caccini, Frescobaldi,
Froberger, Tosi, Quantz, L. Mozart, W. A. Mozart, Hum-
mel, Chopin, and Liszt.

91. Paderewski, Ignacy J. "Rhythm is Life." <u>Music
   Journal</u>, XXI/4 (Apr. 1963) 40-42, 73.
   A discussion of rhythm and tempo rubato from a
pianist's point of view. Emphasizes Chopin's works.

92. Reddick, William J. <u>The Standard Musical Repertoire,
   with Accurate Timings</u>. Garden City, NY: Double-
   day & Co., 1947, 192 p.
   Lists performance time and conductor or performer
for approximately 2000 works, divided into music for orchestra, violin, piano, solo voice, and chorus.
   Review by Donald L. Engle, <u>Notes</u>, V/2 (Mar. 1948)
240-41.

 Sachs, Curt. <u>Rhythm and Tempo: A Study in Music
History</u>. See No. 24.

93. Sternberg, Constantin von. "Tempo Rubato." <u>Musician</u>,
   XVII/8 (Aug. 1912) 524-25.
   Discusses the performance, history, and teaching of
tempo rubato.

94. Wilson, G. Mark. "The Metronome--Its Use and Lim-
   itation." <u>Musician</u>, XIX/9 (Sept. 1914) 578-79.
   Gives a short history of the metronome; cites its
uses and limitations in developing rhythmic sense, technical
skill, and musical interpretation.

Chapter 2

PSYCHOLOGY OF RHYTHM

A. General Materials

      An understanding of the psychology of rhythm in all
of its many aspects is of great importance to composers,
conductors, educators, performers, music students, and lis-
teners alike. In this section are listed secondary source materials: surveys and syntheses of research designed to orient
the reader and to direct him to the actual research itself.
Particularly comprehensive and systematic in approach are
the works by Boring (No. 95), Lundin (No. 101), and Mursell
(No. 105). Works which relate research findings to music
education include those by Biggs (No. 32), Gordon (No. 98),
Lauritzen (No. 226), Mursell (No. 103), Mursell and Glenn
(No. 106), Pickens (No. 391), Seashore (No. 115), and Zimmerman (No. 117). For an extensive discussion of the effect
of rhythm on emotional and intellectual meaning in music see
Meyer (No. 102).

      Biggs, George B. , Jr. "A Suggested Taxonomy of
Music for Music Educators. " See No. 32.

95. Boring, Edwin G. Sensation and Perception in the His-
      tory of Experimental Psychology. New York: D.
      Appleton-Century Co. , 1942, 644 p.

Chapter XV contains a concise history of psychological research in the field of rhythm.

96. Dreikurs, Rudolf. "The Psychological and Philosophical Significance of Rhythm." Bulletin of the National Association for Music Therapy, VI/1 (Jan. 1957) 7-8. Reprinted in X/4 (1961) 8-17.

A synthesis of the psychological literature pertaining to rhythm. Emphasizes the cultural and communicative nature of rhythm and its use as a therapeutic and corrective force in music therapy. A bibliography of thirty-two items is included.

97. Dunlap, Knight. "Rhythm and Time." Psychological Bulletin, VIII (July 1911) 239-42.

A critical review of experiments in rhythm and time including Herbert Woodrow's "A Quantitative Study of Rhythm" (see No. 170) and "The Rôle of Pitch in Rhythm" (see No. 171).

98. Gordon, Edwin. The Psychology of Music Teaching. Englewood Cliffs, NJ: Prentice-Hall, Inc., 1971, 138 p.

The main purpose of this book "... is to provide basic insights into how students learn music."--Preface, p. xi. Chapter V, "Rhythmic Learning," synthesizes research results from forty-five studies which pertain to various aspects of rhythm. Chapter sub-headings indicate the areas discussed: Definition of Rhythm, Organization of Rhythm Patterns, Rhythm Readiness, Rhythm Reading and Writing, and Theory of Rhythm Notation.

Particularly valuable are the criteria given for practical rhythm syllables, procedures for rhythmical development of students with different rhythmic aptitudes in group situations, observations on confusing aspects of meter signatures, and a discussion not indicated by the chapter sub-headings of six small but important points: beamed notation, sightreading rhythms, "shorthand" rhythmic notation, teaching the dotted quarter and eighth rhythm, function of the bar line, and rhythmic interpretation.

The choice of terminology in the section on the organization of rhythm patterns may be open to criticism, as is most certainly the suggestion that a set of rhythm syllables of anonymous (Gordon's?) origin ("1-Ta-Ne-Ta" = ♫♫ and "1-Ba-Bi" = ♫♪) "... are easily articulated with the tongue and therefore can be employed while one plays a wind instrument without necessarily impairing embouchure."--p. 74.

99.   Hartman, James B.   A Gestalt Theory of Musical Per-
      ception.   Ph. D. dissertation, Northwestern Univer-
      sity, 1959, 272 p.;   LC 59-4803;   DA XX/6, 2332.
      Examines various forms of perceptual organization
in the melodic, rhythmic, and harmonic dimensions of music
from the viewpoint of Gestalt psychology.   In the discussion
of rhythmic organization, the nature of rhythmic groups is
considered along with the various types of rhythmic organization to be found in both classical and contemporary music.

100.   Isaacs, Elcanon.   "The Nature of the Rhythmic Exper-
       ience."   Psychological Review, XXVII (July 1920)
       270-99.
       Summarizes sixty-four studies in the field of rhythm.
Notes the objective characteristics of rhythm which are necessary to arouse a serial response.

      Krehbiel, James W.   "Rhythm, Meter and Syncopation."
See No. 18.

      Lauritzen, Adrian R. M.   "Some Psychophysical Im-
plications of Rhythm Pedagogy in the Primary Grades."   See
No. 226.

101.   Lundin, Robert W.   An Objective Psychology of Music.
       2nd ed.   New York: Ronald Press Co., 1967,
       345 p.
       A particularly well-organized, succinct account
which brings Mursell's The Psychology of Music (see No.
105) up to date.   Chapter VII discusses rhythm as a stimulus
and as a response.   Classifies the theories of rhythmic response into three types: instinctive, physiological, and motor.   Maintains that a modified motor theory seems the most
plausible and is closest to the available data.

102.   Meyer, Leonard B.   Emotion and Meaning in Music.
       Chicago: University of Chicago Press, 1956, 307 p.
       Based almost entirely on the theory first advanced
by John Dewey in 1894, which has since become known as
the conflict theory of emotions.   Gives a technical explanation
of how rhythm and the other elements of music arouse and
inhibit tendencies and thereby give rise to emotions.
       Review by Richard S. Hill in Notes, XIV/2 (Mar.
1957) 252-55;   David Kraehenbuehl in Journal of Music
Theory, I/1 (Mar. 1957) 110-12;   Edward A. Lippman in
Musical Quarterly, XLIII/4 (Oct. 1957) 553-57;   Julius
Portnoy in Journal of Aesthetics and Art Criticism, XVI/2
(Dec. 1957) 285-86.

See also No. 34, Grosvenor Cooper and Leonard B.
Meyer, The Rhythmic Structure of Music.

103. Mursell, James L. Principles of Musical Education.
        New York: Macmillan Co. , 1927, 300 p.
        Chapter III, "The Rhythmic Experience in Music:
Its Nature and Training," asserts that to teach rhythm properly, its psychological aspects must be understood. Research
in the psychology of rhythm is discussed generally. The
Jaques-Dalcroze system of eurhythmics is mentioned as being
the best method for training the sense of rhythm.

104. _____. "Psychology of Music." Psychological Bul-
        letin, XXIX (Mar. 1932) 218-41.
        Contains a survey of twenty-nine studies on musical
rhythm.

105. _____. The Psychology of Music. New York:
        W. W. Norton & Co. , Inc. , 1937, 389 p.
        A synthesis and interpretation of 605 research
studies from sources international in scope. Taken together,
the chapters on the perception of rhythm and the structure of
musical rhythm are comprehensive and especially valuable
for utilizing experimental results to explain perception of
rhythm in examples of great music.

106. _____ and Mabelle Glenn. The Psychology of School
        Music Teaching. New York: Silver, Burdett & Co. ,
        1931, 378 p.
        Chapter VII, "Rhythmic Training," discusses the
basic psychology in teaching rhythm, the nature of musical
rhythm, and muscular response to rhythm. Outlines the advantages and disadvantages of using the following "devices"
in the teaching of rhythm: counting, tapping the beat, the
metronome, tapping the phrase rhythm, the use of words,
ensemble experience, and conducting. The Jaques-Dalcroze
system of eurhythmics is offered as the best means of teaching rhythm. A significant bibliography is included.

107. Nichols, Herbert. "The Psychology of Time." Ameri-
        can Journal of Psychology, III (Feb. 1891) 453-529;
        IV (Apr. 1891) 60-112.
        A survey of literature on the nature of time and
rhythm arranged chronologically from Plato's writings to current studies on the psychological aspects of the subject.

108. Pepinsky, Abe. "The Nature of Rhythmic Experience."

Proceedings of the Music Teachers National Association XL (1946) 321-29.

A summary of the important research in rhythmic perception. Modifies Woodrow's findings in "The Role of Pitch in Rhythm" (see No. 171). Finds that periodic pitch variations do have a rhythm-producing influence. Offers observations on the tension existing between tones of different pitch with respect to rhythmic stress.

Pickens, Blanchard. "The Teaching of Rhythm to Instrumental Music Students." See No. 391.

109. Ruckmick, Christian A. "A Bibliography of Rhythm." American Journal of Psychology, XXIV (Oct. 1913) 508-9; XXVI (July 1915) 457-59; XXIX (Apr. 1918) 214-18; XXXV (July 1924) 407-13.

One of the first attempts at compiling a comprehensive bibliography of rhythm materials. Lists 741 items dealing primarily with rhythmical phenomena in the area of psychology, but also includes contributions to the fields of music, pictorial and sculptural art, prosody, pedagogy, dance, physiology, biology, geology, physics, and chemistry. The first section, published in 1913, was originally part of the author's Ph.D. dissertation, "The Rôle of Kinaesthesis in the Perception of Rhythm, with a Bibliography of Rhythm" (see No. 149).

110. _____. "The Nature of the Rhythmic Experience." Proceedings of the Music Teachers National Association, XXXIX (1945) 79-89.

A general discussion of the subject, based on the major research of the author and of Herbert Woodrow.

111. _____. "Rhythm and Its Musical Implications." Proceedings of the Music Teachers National Association, XIX (1924) 53-62.

A survey of the theories of rhythm with an emphasis upon mental characteristics, processes, and effects which exist in the perception of rhythm.

112. _____. "The Rhythmical Experience from a Systematic Point of View." American Journal of Psychology, XXXIX (Dec. 1927) 356-66.

Discusses rhythmic perception in relation to Gestalttheorie, the laws of attention, and the general organization of the mind. Related research is listed.

113.   Seashore, Carl E.   "Motor Ability, Reaction-Time,
            Rhythm, and Time Sense."   University of Iowa
            Studies in Psychology, II (1899) 64-84.
        A statistical, psychological study on the time of
action, simple reaction, discrimination, choice, free and
regulated rhythm in action, and time estimate.

114.   _____.   Psychology of Music.   New York: McGraw-
            Hill Book Co., 1938, 408 p.   Reprinted by Dover
            Publications, Inc., New York, 1967.
        Chapter XII, "Rhythm," is a reprint of the author's
article "The Sense of Rhythm as a Musical Talent" (No. 116).
A brief treatment of the psychology of rhythm is added.

115.   _____.   The Psychology of Musical Talent.   Boston:
            Silver, Burdett & Co., 1919, 288 p.
        Exerted great influence on music educators, espe-
cially those attending the Eastman School of Music ca. 1930-
65, because of its use as required reading for collegiate
courses in the subject.   Chapter IV, "The Sense of Time,"
discusses the measurement and musical significance of the
sense of time and its relation to age, training, intelligence,
and sense of pitch.   Chapter V, "The Sense of Rhythm," is
essentially the same as the author's article, "The Sense of
Rhythm as a Musical Talent" (No. 116).

116.   _____.   The Sense of Rhythm as a Musical Talent."
            Musical Quarterly, IV/4 (Oct. 1918) 507-15.
        Maintains that the ability to perceive rhythm is in-
nate but measurable.   Describes the two fundamental factors
in the perception of rhythm as the "instinctive tendency to
group impressions in hearing" (subjective) and the "capacity
for doing this with precision in time and stress" (objective).
Also outlines five fundamental capacities for the perception
of rhythm: the sense of time, the sense of intensity, auditory
imagery, motor imagery, and motor impulse.

117.   Zimmerman, Marilyn P.   Musical Characteristics of
            Children.   From Research to the Music Classroom
            Series, No. 1.   Washington, DC: Music Educators
            National Conference, 1971, 32 p.
        This monograph, which treats the basic elements of
music, is included here for its valuable summary of selected
research findings on the perceptual, conceptual, affective, and
manipulative development of rhythm in children.   Shows how
the findings may be applied by the music teacher to the
teaching-learning process.   A bibliography of forty-one items
of research is included.

B. Perception of Rhythm

In the psychological studies completed around the
end of the 19th century, the sense of rhythm was thought to
be closely connected with the sense of time or duration.
More recent investigations have shown that the sense of
rhythm is independent from that of time. However, representative studies which deal with rhythm, with time, and
with a combination of rhythm and time are included here for
the sake of completeness.

The studies in this section were published during
the period of 1886 to 1971 and investigate the effect produced
by and the response to rhythm. Perhaps the most important
studies, as evidenced by their influence on other research
and on writers such as Leonard B. Meyer in Emotion and
Meaning in Music (No. 102), are those by Ruckmick (No.
150), Stetson (No. 159), and Woodrow (No. 170); this fact
has warranted a lengthier annotation for these items. For
research especially applicable to the field of music education,
see Petzold (No. 146).

118. Bolton, Thaddeus L. "On the Discrimination of Groups
      of Rapid Clicks." American Journal of Psychology,
      V (Apr. 1893) 294-310.
      Discusses the abilities of subjects to discriminate
the number of discrete clicks in small and large groups, the
number of clicks at various speeds, and the presence of more
or fewer clicks in successive groups.

119. _____. "Rhythm." American Journal of Psychology,
      VI (Jan. 1894) 145-238.
      After a preliminary thirty-three page discussion of
rhythms in nature, physiological rhythms, attention and per-
iodicity, rhythmic speech, time-relations, intensity of sounds,
qualities of sounds, the emotional effects of rhythm upon sav-
ages and children, and the place of rhythm in music and
poetry, Bolton records the results of his own experiments

concerning the effects of intensity and duration upon grouping.
Asserts that changes in a series of impressions produce corresponding changes in the intensity of the sensation, which
then find expression in different degrees of muscular activity.
States the following general principle:

> In a series of auditory impressions, any regu-
> larly recurrent impression which is different
> from the rest, subordinates the other impressions
> to it in such a way that they fall together in
> groups. If the recurrent difference is one of
> intensity, the strongest impression comes first
> in the group and the weaker ones after. If the
> recurrent difference is one of duration, the
> longest impression comes last. --p. 232.

Also finds that all rhythmical groups are separated
by intervals subjectively longer than the intervals within the
groups, even though all the intervals are objectively equal.
See also No. 170, Herbert A. Woodrow, "A Quantitative Study of Rhythm."

120. Bond, Marjorie H. "Rhythmic Perception and Gross
      Motor Performance." Unpublished Ph. D. disserta-
      tion, University of Southern California, 1958, 136 p.

121. Broman, Keith L.   The Effects of Subjective Rhythmic
      Grouping Observed Under the Influence of Variable
      Rates, Frequencies, Numbers, and Tonal Stimuli.
      Ph. D. dissertation, Indiana University, 1956, 164 p.;
      LC 56-5348; DA XVI/12, 2535.
      Determines the effect of rate, pitch, number of
stimuli, and melodic patterns on subjective rhythmic grouping.
Thirty college music majors and 245 matriculating college
freshmen were required to subjectively organize stimuli by
indicating with a vertical stroke those dots in a series which
appeared to be accented.   Each dot on the answer sheet cor-
responded to one tone of the aural stimuli.

122. Buck, Nadine. "Comparison of Two Methods of Test-
      ing Response to Auditory Rhythms." Research
      Quarterly, VII (Oct. 1936) 36-45.
      Compares two methods of measuring responses to
aurally presented rhythmic figures: tapping the rhythm following its presentation, and reproducing the figure graphically
using short and long dashes.   Finds that writing the rhythm
is six times more difficult than tapping it, and that the
written responses become a measure of the conscious perception of rhythm.

123. Creelman, Carleton D. Human Discrimination of Audi-
        tory Duration. Ph. D. dissertation, University of
        Michigan, 1961, 66 p. ; LC 61-1733; DA XXII/1,
        331.
        Reports on a series of related experiments which
measured the ability of paid observers to discriminate durations of auditory signals. Two sine-wave signals differing
only in duration were presented in random order on each
trial, and the observers' task was to determine whether the
longer signal had occurred first or second.

124. DeGraff, Lula H. "The Norms of the Sensitiveness to
        Rhythm." Unpublished M. A. thesis, University of
        Iowa, 1924, 49 p.
        Working with fifth graders, eighth graders, and
adults, DeGraff found that there is low correlation between
the perception of rhythm and tonal memory, sense of time,
and sense of intensity. The factors of age, sex, and training were found to have little influence on rhythmical perception. Concludes that rhythm is an innate capacity depending
largely upon mental and physiological processes.

125. Dittemore, Edgar E. "An Investigation of Some Mu-
        sical Capabilities of Elementary School Students."
        University of Iowa Studies in the Psychology of
        Music, VI (1970) 1-44.
        Investigates various melodic, rhythmic, and har-
monic capabilities manifest at different grade levels in average elementary school students. The sequence for the development of rhythmic capability is: 1) ability to perform in
"duple" and "triple" meter, 2) ability to perform "mixed"
meter, and 3) ability to perform "unusual" meter.
        See also No. 98, Edwin Gordon, The Psychology of
Music Teaching, Chapter V.

126. Gardner, Bruce D. and Marcia H. Rosenbusch. "Re-
        production of Visual and Auditory Rhythm Patterns
        by Children." Perception and Motor Skills, XXVI/
        3, Part II (1968) 1271-76.
        Studied developmental patterns in rhythm percep-
        tion in 2 modalities. 80 5-13 yr. old children
        were assigned to either the visual or auditory
        task of reproducing 4 different rhythm patterns.
        Analysis was done for [sense] modality, age,
        and the interaction of age with modality. There
        were pronounced effects of modality on perfor-
        mance, with no interaction between age and

modality. Results are compared with those from
other studies concerned with time and rhythm
perception and are discussed in terms of the developmental implications. The effect of variance
within rhythm patterns and between components is
also discussed. --RILM Abstracts, II/2 (May-
Aug. 1968) 212.

127. Gardner, Howard. "Children's Duplication of Rhythmic
        Patterns." Journal of Research in Music Education,
        XIX/3 (Fall 1971) 355-60.
        Investigates the ability of first, third, and sixth
grade children to imitate rhythm patterns consisting of from
four to eight taps. Implications of the findings for music
education are given.

128. Gaston, Everett [Thayer]. "Dynamic Music Factors
        in Mood Change." Music Educators Journal,
        XXXVII/4 (Feb. 1951) 42-44.
        A discussion in layman's terms of the affective
quality of rhythm and tempo.

129. Griesemer, John E. "Aural, Visual, and Tactual
        Sensitivity to Rhythm." Unpublished M.S. thesis,
        Illinois State Normal University, 1958, 38 p.
        The perception of rhythm patterns by means of
        the aural, visual, and tactual senses was studied
        by administering the Seashore rhythm test to
        fifty-two subjects with mechanisms designed to
        produce sounds, light-blinks, and tapping-pres-
        sures. The scores achieved by these subjects
        for each of the three senses were compared with
        relation to order of presentation of the tests;
        age and musical background; sex; and cultural,
        economic, and intellectual influences. [Results]
        ... indicate that the order of ability of the three
        sense modalities tested is aural first, tactual
        second, and visual last. --p. 34.

130. Hall, G. Stanley and Joseph Jastrow. "Studies in
        Rhythm." Mind, XI (Jan. 1886) 54-62.
        Presents three studies which determine: 1) the
largest number of beats that can be accurately counted during
a given interval of time, 2) the smallest deviation in a series
of time intervals that can be observed, and 3) the illusion of
length in sound-filled intervals as opposed to silent intervals.

131. Hanson, Howard. "Some Objective Studies of Rhythm
      in Music." American Journal of Psychiatry, CI/3
      (Nov. 1944) 364-69.
      Surveys the role tempo, dynamic accent, metric
accent, and metric subdivision play in creating emotional tension in music. Musical examples by Mozart, Beethoven,
Handel, Haydn, J. Braham, and Z. Confrey are given. Hanson objects to the rhythm of the "violent boogie-woogie" and
warns of its "nerve-wracking" effects.

132. Heinlein, Christian P. "A New Method of Studying the
      Rhythmic Responses of Children, Together with an
      Evaluation of the Method of Simple Observation."
      Pedagogical Seminary and Journal of Genetic Psy-
      chology, XXXVI (June 1929) 205-228.
      Eight kindergarten age children were told to walk
in time to music on a runway that had electric contacts designed to record their steps. The beat of the music to which
they were listening was also recorded at the same time.
Only one child demonstrated coordination between the walking
movements and the musical beat. Findings indicate that
adult observers are prone to think the children are keeping
time with the rhythm when this does not occur.

133. Hevner, Kate. "Experimental Studies of the Elements
      of Expression in Music." American Journal of
      Psychology, XLVIII (Apr. 1936) 246-68.
      Demonstrates the relative importance of mode,
rhythm, harmony, and melody on the affective value (meaning and character) of music. Two versions of musical compositions were prepared which differed in one respect only,
e. g. , the rhythm. It was found that firm rhythms were described as vigorous and dignified; flowing rhythms as happy,
graceful, dreamy, and tender; and neither was particularly
useful in determining such characteristics as excitement,
serenity, and satisfaction.
      See also No. 185, Kate Hevner, "The Affective
Value of Pitch and Tempo in Music."

134. Houts, Earl. A Controlled Experimental Study to De-
      termine Growth in the Perception-Response of Ele-
      mentary Music Rhythms Using Kinesthesis. Ed. D.
      dissertation, Colorado State College of Education,
      1956, 199 p.
      Tests and proves the hypothesis that rhythmic im-
pressions are more effectively perceived as ordered kinesthetic cues and aural and visual forms rather than their being
"reasoned out" through counting.

135. Husband, Richard M. "The Effects of Musical Rhythm
        and Pure Rhythms on Bodily Sway." Journal of
        General Psychology, XI (Oct. 1934) 328-36.
        Determines the effects of rhythmic patterns embodied
in music and "pure" rhythmic patterns produced by a buzzer
upon the unconscious sway of the body as a subject stands
erect with his eyes closed. The conclusion that musical
rhythms produced three times as much sway than did pure
rhythms is open to question because identical rhythmic patterns were not used in the two cases. One hundred and
fifty-six subjects were involved.

136. Jersild, Arthur T. and Sylvia F. Beinstock. Develop-
        ment of Rhythm in Young Children. New York:
        Bureau of Publications, Teachers College, Columbia
        University, 1935, 97 p.
        Investigates the ability of pre-school children to
keep time to music by tapping and walking, and to respond
to various tempi and meters. Results showed significant differences due to age, no differences due to sex, and that children are better able to keep time to music played at fast
tempi.

137. MacDougall, Robert. "The Affective Quality of Audi-
        tory Rhythm in Its Relation to Objective Forms."
        Psychological Review, X (Jan. 1903) 15-36.
        Discusses eleven objective factors upon which the
character and intensity of satisfaction and dissatisfaction in
a rhythmical sequence depend.

138. _____. "The Relation of Auditory Rhythm to Ner-
        vous Discharge." Psychological Review, IX (Sept.
        1902) 460-80.
        Conclusions drawn from experiments on typical con-
vulsive movements found among the insane indicate that normal people (including musical artists) perceive auditory, visual, or kinesthetic stimuli as being rhythmically grouped only
when the rate at which they are received corresponds to the
basic rate of the waves of nervous discharge.
        See critical comments by Lundin in An Objective
Psychology of Music (No. 101), p. 119.

139. _____. "Rhythm, Time and Number." American
        Journal of Psychology, XIII (Jan. 1902) 88-97.
        A survey of the literature on the psychology of
rhythm with a presentation of results obtained on an experiment dealing with the perception of varying numbers of

auditory stimuli occurring in groups.

140. _____ . "The Structure of Simple Rhythm Forms."
        Psychological Review, Monograph Supplements,
        IV/17 (1903) 309-412.
        Presents a discussion of sound quality as it affects
the perception of rhythmical groups. Findings show that a
loud sound tends to decrease the apparent duration of the interval following it and to increase the apparent duration of the
interval preceding it. The strength of this effect was measured by shortening the objective duration of the interval immediately preceding a loud sound until a point was reached
where the rhythm of the group was destroyed. This was
called the "indifference point." Also asserts that in order
for a rhythm to be perceived, it must be felt kinesthetically.
        See the critical review by Herbert A. Woodrow in
"A Quantitative Study of Rhythm" (No. 170).

141. Mainwaring, James. "Experiments on the Analysis of
        Cognitive Processes Involved in Musical Ability and
        in Musical Education." British Journal of Educa-
        tional Psychology, I (June 1931) 180-203.
        A study of children between the ages of nine and
one-half and eleven and one-half which reports no consistent
relationship between perception of pitch differences and perception of rhythmic patterns. Findings indicate that age is
an important factor in the development of rhythm.

142. _____ . "Psychological Factors in the Teaching of
        Music." British Journal of Educational Psychology,
        XXI (1951) 105-21, 199-213.
        Describes how metrical and rhythmic concepts are
formed, developed, and associated with their respective symbols of notation. Maintains that the natural feeling for pulse
is duple and discusses bodily movement, French time-names,
anacrustic rhythmic figures, and dotted notes. Concurs with
Buck (see No. 122) in stating that "... whereas no analytical
knowledge is needed for the imitative reproduction of music,
conceptual analysis becomes necessary immediately [sic]
musical thoughts have to be directly transcribed to paper."--
p. 109.

        McEwen, Sir John B. The Thought in Music: An
Enquiry into the Principles of Musical Rhythm, Phrasing and
Expression. See No. 21.

143. Miner, James B. "Motor, Visual, and Applied

Rhythms." Psychological Review, Monograph
Supplements, V/21 (1903) 1-106.
Concludes that the experience of rhythm in the field
of vision is identical in its essentials with that in the auditory
field.
See the critical review by Herbert A. Woodrow in
"A Quantitative Study of Rhythm" (No. 170).

144. Morton, W. B. "Some Measurements of the Accuracy
of the Time-Intervals in Playing a Keyed Instrument." British Journal of Psychology, X (1919-
1920) 194-98.
An admittedly carelessly arranged experiment to
determine the degree of accuracy attained by pianists in the
rhythmical performance of "three against two." Also examines the influence of accent on the spacing of the notes.

145. Nelson, Mabel L. "The Effect of Subdivisions on the
Visual Estimate of Time." Psychological Review,
IX (Sept. 1902) 447-59.
Results indicate that there exists "... in intervals
of time ranging from 3 to 60 seconds, evidence of a temporal
illusion very similar to the space illusion of sight. Both in
time and in visual space, when there is more than a single
division, the filled stretch is overestimated."--pp. 458-59.
However, a single division does not shorten the temporal estimate.

146. Petzold, Robert G. Auditory Perception of Musical
Sounds by Children in the First Six Grades. U. S.
Office of Education Cooperative Research Project
No. 1051, University of Wisconsin, 1966, 277 p. ;
ED 010 297.
This five-year research project (1960-1965) is a
continuation of a pilot study which dealt with the auditory perception of the melodic element of music. The project consists of a longitudinal study of three groups of children and
a series of one-year pilot studies dealing with rhythm, tim-
bre, and harmony. Individual testing required each child to
make an overt musical response to an aural presentation of
the test item.
In the area of rhythm, tests were constructed which
determined what relationships exist between the accuracy with
which children perceive and respond to rhythmic patterns
when the modes of aural presentation are varied, when the
modes of response are varied, and when the patterns vary
as to meter, length, and complexity. In general, it was

found that the ability to imitate the presentation of certain
musical ideas was not a measure of the understanding of
such ideas.
       See also abstract in Research in Education, II/4
(Apr. 1967) 4.
       See also Robert G. Petzold, Development of Audi-
tory Perception of Musical Sounds by Children in the First
Six Grades, (Madison: University of Wisconsin, 1960);
Robert G. Petzold, "The Development of Auditory Perception
of Musical Sounds by Children in the First Six Grades,"
Journal of Research in Music Education, XI/1 (Spring 1963)
21-43; and Robert G. Petzold, "Auditory Perception by
Children," Journal of Research in Music Education, XVII/1
(Spring 1969) 82-87.

            Pottenger, Harold P.   An Analysis of Rhythm Reading
Skill. See No. 241.

147.   Ross, Felix B.   "The Measurement of Time-Sense as
            an Element in the Sense of Rhythm." Psychological
            Review, Monograph Supplements, XVI/69 (1914)
            166-72.
       Reports on an experiment in which the interval be-
tween clicks was shortened to determine if subjects could se-
lect the shortened interval.

148.   Rowland, Eleanor H.   "The Aesthetics of Repeated
            Space Forms." Harvard Studies in Psychology, II
            (1906) 193-268.
       Compares the visual perception of object repetition
to auditory rhythmic perception. Ten basic conclusions are
drawn which are shown to be valid by demonstrating that they
have been exemplified in European architecture which has
been universally accepted as aesthetically beautiful.

149.   Ruckmick, Christian A.   "The Rôle of Kinaesthesis in
            the Perception of Rhythm, with a Bibliography of
            Rhythm." Unpublished Ph.D. dissertation, Cornell
            University, 1913.

150.   _____. "The Rôle of Kinaesthesis in the Perception
            of Rhythm, with a Bibliography of Rhythm." Amer-
            ican Journal of Psychology, XXIV (July 1913) 305-
            59; XXIV (Oct. 1913) 508-19.
       This is Ruckmick's Ph.D. dissertation (see No.
149).
       Concludes that:

... whatever material was presented for rhyth-
misation (equal and equally spaced sounds for
subjective rhythm; sounds of different intensities;
tones objectively varying only in duration, in intensity, in pitch; flashes of light differing in
intensity), kinaesthesis was essential for the es-
tablishment of a rhythmical perception. That
perception once established, however, rhythm
might be consciously carried, in the absence of
any sort of kinaesthesis, by auditory or visual
processes. --p. 359.
See also No. 109, Christian A. Ruckmick, "A Bibliography of Rhythm."

151. _____. "Visual Rhythm." Studies in Psychology:
       Titchener Commemorative Volume. Worcester,
       MA: Louis N. Wilson Co. , pp. 231-54.
       Experiments using flashing lights as stimuli elicited
responses which showed that visual rhythm can be perceived.

152. Ruppenthal, Wayne. "A Study of the Subjective Organ-
       ization of Rhythm in Musical Context as Indicated
       by Motor Activity." Unpublished M. M. Ed. thesis,
       University of Kansas, 1948.

153. Sears, Charles H. "A Contribution to the Psychology
       of Rhythm." American Journal of Psychology,
       XIII (Jan. 1902) 28-61.
       An experimental study of the rhythmical discrepan-
cies in the performances of four subjects playing seven hymns
on an organ. Includes a survey of related literature.

154. Seashore, Robert H. "An Experimental and Theoretical
       Analysis of Fine Motor Skills." American Journal
       of Psychology, LIII (Jan. 1940) 86-98.
           ... studies of threshold activities of a single
       sense-field have shown in the case of audition
       that there is no single sense of hearing, but
       rather a series of nearly specific acuities (e. g.
       pitch, intensity, time). --p. 98.

155. Simpson, Shirley E. "Development and Validation of
       an Objective Measure of Locomotor Response to
       Auditory Rhythmic Stimuli." Research Quarterly,
       XXIX (Oct. 1958) 342-48.
       An instrument called the Rhythmeter which makes
objective measurements of locomotor response to auditory

rhythmic stimuli was developed and validated. It was found
that sensory and motor responses are not similar either
within individuals or among groups. States that "... rhythm
is kinesthetic in that it must be felt by the individual, and it
is instinctive in that all individuals are able to feel and respond to rhythmic stimulation."--p. 342.

156.   Sloan, Muriel R.   A Comparison of Group Responses
           to Auditory, Visual, and Kinesthetic Rhythms.
           Ph. D. dissertation, University of Wisconsin, 1958,
           318 p. ;   LC 58-2576;   DA XIX/2, 269.
           Four groups of subjects representing extremes of
skill and experience were used in an exploration into the relationship of responses to rhythms (defined as equally spaced
series of stimuli) and motor skill.   The study compares responses to kinesthetic rhythms with responses to auditory and
visual rhythms, investigates the relationship of responses to
auditory, visual, and kinesthetic rhythms to opposite extremes
of skill and/or experience in sports and dance, and compares
responses to kinesthetic rhythms produced through different
movement sources.

157.   Spencer, Gary D.   The Relationship of Reading to
           Auditory Discrimination of Differences in Rhythm,
           Pitch, and Tonal Sequence.   Ed. D. dissertation,
           Arizona State University, 1964, 97 p. ;   LC 64-
           12,827;   DA XXVI/2, 912.
           Describes relationships that existed between reading
achievement and auditory discrimination in children in the
third, fifth, and eighth grades in two schools of socio-economic
extremes.   Findings indicate no statistically significant correlation between reading achievement and the rhythm test
given.

158.   Squire, C. R.   "A Genetic Study of Rhythm."   Ameri-
           can Journal of Psychology, XII (July 1901) 492-589.
           Attempts to determine the essential constituents of
rhythm.   Rhythmical forms are classified in the order of
their psychological complexity.   Duple grouping of pulses is
preferred over triple grouping.   Squire asserts that a rhythm
becomes unpleasant when it exceeds the natural rate of the
individual or when it is too complex to be readily perceived.
           "The great pleasure which children find in rhythm
is due to the efficacy of rhythm to set up vibrations in other
organs of the body, and the consequent harmonious activity
of the several bodily organs."--p. 588.

159.   Stetson, R. B.   "A Motor Theory of Rhythm and Dis-
       crete Succession." Psychological Review, XII
       (1905) 250-70, 293-350.
       A study of major importance on the objective and
subjective conditions of rhythm. Asserts that "Every sound
must be assumed to cause a movement involving the general
musculature."--p. 307. Two of the most common illusions
of rhythmic perception, "subjective accentuation" and "temporal displacement," are discussed.
            Concerning subjective accentuation, the study states
that

            In case the sound which falls on the accented
            beat does not have an intensity corresponding to
            the intensity of the beat, the movement-cycle it-
            self contributes the requisite vividness.--p. 307.
            Concerning temporal displacement, the study states
that

            The position in the objective time series in which
            the sounds occur may be modified by the rhythm
            process.... If a series of equidistant sounds
            like the ticks of a metronome are heard, the ob-
            server may phrase them into iambs, trochees,
            or dactyls, as he chooses. To the ear, the
            choice seems to affect merely the vividness of
            the beats. But if the observer taps a key at
            each beat of the metronome, it will be found
            that in the case of the iamb he always misplaces
            the beats; often the same thing happens in the
            case of the trochee and dactyl. Because of the
            influence of the rhythm process, the observer
            does not hear the beats where they actually occur.
            In the case of the iamb he always hears the beat
            which he makes subordinate nearer the accented
            beat than it actually is in the objective clicking
            of the metronome.--p. 308.

160.   _____ and T. E. Tuthill. "Measurements of Rhyth-
       mic Unit Groups at Different Tempos." Psychological
       Monographs, XXXII/145 (1923) 41-51.
       An experiment with highly trained musicians who
tapped iambs and dactyls in addition to other rhythmic sequences. Regardless of the tempi, strong beats were prolonged and weak beats were abbreviated.
            Further substantiates the author's earlier research,
"A Motor Theory of Rhythm and Discrete Succession" (No.
159).

161. Swindle, P. F. "On the Inheritance of Rhythm."
          American Journal of Psychology, XXIV (Apr. 1913)
          180-203.
          Reviews the research on rhythm and asserts that
rhythm is acquired and not inherited by an individual. Finds
that in the development of rhythm, the motor activity of the
skeletal muscles plays the most important role. The Jacques-
Dalcroze method of eurhythmics is discussed in light of research results.

162. Teague, Webster W. The Untrained Listener's Beat
          Response to Auditory Musical Stimuli. Ph. D. dis-
          sertation, Florida State University, 1968, 91 p. ;
          LC 69-16,397; DA XXX/4A, 1592.
          Investigates the nature of beat response in the un-
trained listener (defined as one who does not read music notation, has not received formal musical instruction, and has
not participated in a performing musical organization). Subjects were required to beat time to music by tapping on a
woodblock. According to the author, some traditional assump-
tions are challenged by the findings of the study: 1) propen-
sity toward beat response is not categorically uniform,
2) promptness of response to successive hearings of a given
musical passage does not remain constant, and 3) responses
to the same musical passage vary greatly from one person
to another.
          The small sample of only fifteen college students
used in the study raises some doubt as to the validity and
reliability of these findings.

163. Thackray, Rupert. An Investigation into Rhythmic
          Abilities. London: Novello & Co. , Ltd. , 1969,
          47 p.
          Investigates rhythmic perception, performance, and
movement. Findings indicate that although rhythmic ability is
complex, there is a common factor running through all the
forms of rhythmic activity which may be defined as the ability
to perceive rhythmic structures in respect to the three elements of timing, duration, and intensity, and the ability to
perform rhythmic movements in which these elements are
clearly defined.

164. _____ . "Rhythmic Abilities and Their Measure-
          ment." Journal of Research in Music Education,
          XVII/1 (Spring 1969) 144-48.
          Included as part of the author's An Investigation
into Rhythmic Abilities (No. 163).

165.   Weaver, H. E.   "Syncopation: A Study of Musical
          Rhythms."   Journal of General Psychology, XX
          (Apr. 1939) 409-29.
             A review of the motor theory of rhythm as it ap-
plies to syncopation.   Ten well-trained musicians used in a
study on simultaneous finger and foot tapping showed a marked
tendency to perceive syncopated notes as emphasized.

166.   Weigl, Vally.   "About Rhythm and Its Effects on Kinetic
          Impulses."   National Association for Music Therapy
          Bulletin, X/2 (May 1961) 9-11.
             Discusses the following effects of rhythm in music
therapy: soothing and comforting effect, physical and emotional stimulation, reduction of tension, feeling of security
and self-confidence, overcoming of fatigue, prolonged attention span, improved working capacity, expression of early
memories, facilitation of social integration.

167.   Whitson, Thomas C.   "A Study of Rhythm Perception
          at the Junior High School Level."   Unpublished
          M. M. thesis, University of Texas, 1951.

168.   Williams, Harold M.   "The Measurement of Musical
          Development: I.   Studies in the Measurement of
          Musical Development."   University of Iowa Studies
          in Child Welfare, VII/1 (Jan. 1932) 11-107.
             Analyzes the development of rhythm in pre-school
children.   States that rhythm is essentially kinesthetic and
motor in nature and evaluates testing techniques for measuring the sense of rhythm.

169.   Wilson, Katharine M.   "What is Rhythm?"   Music and
          Letters, VIII/1 (Jan. 1927) 2-12.
             Considers the roles of emotion, attention span, and
kinesthesis in the perception of musical and poetical rhythm.

170.   Woodrow, Herbert A.   "A Quantitative Study of Rhythm."
          Archives of Psychology, No. 14.   (June 1909) 1-66.
             A study of major importance on the effect of varia-
tions in intensity, rate, and duration upon the perception of
rhythm.   Confirms the experiments of Bolton (see No. 119)
and MacDougall (see No. 140).
                   Four generalizations are stated:
                   1)   With an increase in the ratio of the intensity
                   of the louder sound to that of the weaker, there
                   is an increase, first rapid and then slow, in the
                   tendency of the more intense sound to begin the
                   group. . . .

2) With an increase in the ratio of the duration
of the longer sound to that of the shorter, there
is an increase in the tendency of the longer
sound to end the group or a decrease in its tendency to begin the group....
3) With a constant ratio between the durations
of the sounds, as their absolute duration in-
creases, there is a decrease in the tendency of
the longer sound to begin the group or an increase in its tendency to end the group....
4) The interval preceding the regularly recur-
rent more intense sound or the regularly recur-
rent shorter sound is relatively overestimated
....--pp. 64-66.
These principles are graphically illustrated by
Boring in Sensation and Perception in the History of Experimental Psychology (No. 95), pp. 585-86.

171. _____. "The Rôle of Pitch in Rhythm." Psychological Review, XVIII (Jan. 1911) 54-77.
Reaffirms the author's previous findings in "A
Quantitative Study of Rhythm" (No. 170). Asserts that intensity has a group-beginning effect and duration has a group-
ending effect. Shows that a periodic variation in pitch does
not produce a rhythmic effect. However, Pepinsky gives evidence to the contrary in "The Nature of Rhythmic Experience"
(No. 108).

C. Effect of Training on Rhythmic Perception

This section contains studies on the effect of var-

ious types of training on the perception of rhythm. Also in-

cluded are studies which developed devices and techniques for

measuring this effect. Comparatively few studies in this

area exist--a surprising fact in view of the important impli-

cations it holds for music education. The dissertations of

Coffman (No. 173) and Groves (No. 176) represent the most

recent and perhaps most significant research in this area.

172. Baugh, Elizabeth. "Development of Rhythm Perception
through Training." Unpublished M. A. thesis, Ohio
State University, 1928, 32 p.

An early study which uses Klauer's findings (see
No. 178) as a basis and obtains similar results experimenting
with children in the upper elementary and junior high school
grades.   Concludes that "... rhythm perception cannot be increased by training, but develops inherently. "--p. 30.

173.   Coffman, Ashley R.   "The Effect of Training on Rhythm
            Discrimination and Rhythmic Action. " Unpublished
            Ph. D. dissertation, School of Music, Northwestern
            University, 1949, 106 p.
        Selected junior high school and college students with
low scores in Series A and B of the Seashore Rhythm Discrimination Tests were given various types of rhythmic training, including eurhythmics.   Upon retesting, the trained subjects made significant improvement in their rhythmic discrimination while the control subjects showed no significant improvement.
        Review by Alan H. Drake in Council for Research
in Music Education Bulletin, No. 7 (Spring 1966) 83-87.

174.   _____.   "Is Rhythm Subject to Training?"   School
            Musician, XXI (Sept. 1949) 14, 45.
        Reports results similar to those noted in the au-
thor's dissertation, "The Effect of Training on Rhythm Discrimination and Rhythmic Action" (No. 173).   See also the
critical comments by Lundin in An Objective Psychology of
Music (No. 101), p. 114.

175.   _____.   "Teaching Rhythm. "   Southwestern Musician,
            XX (Mar. 1954) 8.

176.   Groves, William C.   Rhythmic Training and Its Rela-
            tionship to the Synchronization of Motor-Rhythmic
            Responses.   Ed. D. dissertation, University of
            Arkansas, 1966, 100 p. ;   LC 66-7037; DA XXVII/
            3A, 702.
        Finds that rhythmic training has no effect upon the
ability of children in the lower elementary school grades to
synchronize motor-rhythmic responses with rhythmic stimuli.
No significant relationship was found between the home-musical
background, sex, or personal-social adjustment of a student
and his rhythmic-synchronization ability.   The student's motor
ability, age, and grade level were significant factors in this
relationship.

177.   _____.   "Rhythmic Training and Its Relationship to
            the Synchronization of Motor-Rhythmic Responses. "

Journal of Research in Music Education, XVII/4
(Winter 1969) 408-15.
Based upon the author's Ed. D. dissertation of the
same title (see No. 176).

178.   Klauer, Neomi J.   "The Effect of Training in Rhythm
       upon Rhythmic Discrimination in the Intermediate
       Grades."   Unpublished M. A. thesis, University of
       Iowa, 1924, 32 p.
Finds that rhythmic discrimination as measured by
the Seashore rhythm test is not affected to any great extent
by training.

179.   Nielson, James T.   "The Effect of Training on Motor
       Rhythm."   Unpublished M. A. thesis, State Univer-
       sity of Iowa, 1928, 26 p.
Investigates the effect of training on the ability of
forty college students to imitate simple rhythmic patterns by
tapping them on a telegraph key.   Attempts to improve and
further standardize the measures of rhythmic auditory-motor
coordination which were formulated by Robert H. Seashore in
"Studies in Motor Rhythm" (No. 180).

       Seashore, Carl E.   The Psychology of Musical Talent.
See No. 115.

180.   Seashore, Robert H.   "Studies in Motor Rhythm."
       Unpublished Ph. D. dissertation, University of Iowa,
       1925, 80 p.
       Develops a measure of temporal precision in rhyth-
mic auditory-motor coordination and sets standards for eighth-
grade children and adults as an index to individual success
and ability to profit by training in rhythmic action such as
musical performance.   Finds that
            ... the liminal discrimination of small intervals
            of sound is of less importance to rhythm than
            the supra-liminal proficiency [termed kinaesthetic
            memory] in taking and retaining a muscular set
            of the pattern as a whole for a sufficient length
            of time to reproduce it or compare it with a
            second presentation. --p. 75.
       See also No. 179, James T. Nielson, "The Effect
of Training on Motor Rhythm."

181.   Seltzer, Seraphine S.   "A Measure of the Singing and
       Rhythmic Development of Preschool Children."
       Journal of Educational Psychology, XXVII (1936)
       417-24.

The purpose of this study was to devise a measure, simple to understand and use, with which
the musical development of preschool children,
specifically their singing and rhythmic development, could be evaluated. --p. 417.
Each child was evaluated by means of a question-
naire which was filled out according to the opinions of the
rater.

182.   Sievers, Clement H.   "The Measurement of Musical
        Development: II.   A Study of Rhythmic Performance
        with Special Consideration of the Factors Involved
        in the Formation of a Scale for Measuring Rhythmic
        Ability."   University of Iowa Studies in Child Wel-
        fare, VII/1 (Jan. 1932) 111-72.
        Investigates the factor of difficulty in the motor
rhythmic performance of elementary school children and develops a preliminary form of a scale for measuring rhythmic
ability.
        See also abstract in Erwin H. Schneider and Henry
L. Cady, Evaluation and Synthesis of Research Studies ... ,
pp. 445-46.

D.   Perception of Tempo

        The literature in this section deals primarily with

tempo preferences and the affective or expressive properties

of tempo.   Independent researchers working with the same

general problems have arrived at similar findings: compare

Cort (No. 183) with Hevner (No. 185); Farnsworth, Block,

and Waterman (No. 184) with Lund (No. 187).   Judging from

the amount of existing research, this area, like the previous

one, is relatively unexplored.

183.   Cort, Henry R. , Jr.   Tempo and Expressive Properties
        of Auditory Figures: A Psychophysical Study. Ph. D.
        dissertation, Cornell University, 1960, 102 p. ;
        LC 60-6499; DA XXI/7, 2011.
        Supports the proposed hypothesis that tempo affects
the expressive properties of auditory figures.   Subjects described two "pure-tone" melodies that varied in tempo and

musical mode by rating them in terms of eight categories of emotional expression.

184. Farnsworth, Paul R. ; Harold A. Block; and Ward C.
       Waterman. "Absolute Tempo." Journal of General
       Psychology, X (1934) 230-33.
           Investigates the tempo preferences of college stu-
dents. Blindfolded subjects were asked to position the speed
lever of a player-piano so that the tempi of compositions being played (waltz and fox-trot) were considered proper. Results seem to indicate the existence of a controlling "absolute
tempo" of approximately 120 pulses per minute.
           This study was repeated by Lund five years later.
See No. 187, "An Analysis of the 'True Beat' in Music."

       Gaston, Everett [Thayer]. "Dynamic Music Factors in
Mood Change." See No. 128.

       Hanson, Howard. "Some Objective Studies of Rhythm
in Music." See No. 131.

185. Hevner, Kate. "The Affective Value of Pitch and
       Tempo in Music." American Journal of Psychology,
       XLIX (Oct. 1937) 621-30.
           An account of two experiments dealing with pitch
and tempo which complete a series of six studies on expressiveness in music. Summarizes the findings from the whole
series. The previous experiments determined the affective
value of the major versus the minor mode, ascending versus
descending melody, firm versus flowing rhythms, and modern
dissonant harmonies versus classical consonance. In relation
to these four variables, pitch and tempo are shown to be of
the greatest importance in carrying the expressiveness in
music, with tempo playing the largest part of any of these
factors.
           See also No. 133, Kate Hevner, "Experimental
Studies of the Elements of Expression in Music."

186. Hodgson, Walter. "Absolute Tempo: Its Existence,
       Extent, and Possible Explanation." Proceedings of
       the Music Teachers National Association, XLIII
       (1951) 158-69.
           Using the favorably known and carefully selected
           recordings known as the Carnegie set, the ...
           writer measured the principal tempo of every
           third record in the set. Of the 243 measure-
           ments made, almost half fell in the narrow

range between 60 and 70 beats per minute, which
indicates a strong preference of tempo. Attempts
to explain this preference upon such rhythms as
that of heartbeat during sleep (approximately 65)
evidently will prove fruitless, since the mecha-
nism of our time sense seems ultimately to depend upon certain master chemical reactions,
concerning which our knowledge is still too
limited. --p. 169.

Jersild, Arthur T. and Sylvia F. Beinstock.   Development of Rhythm in Young Children.   See No. 136.

187.   Lund, Max W.   "An Analysis of the 'True Beat' in
        Music."   Unpublished Ph. D. dissertation, Stanford
        University, 1939.
        Investigates the tempo preferences of college stu-
dents and reports that preferred tempi for the waltz and fox-
trot are somewhat faster than the findings of Farnsworth,
Block, and Waterman in "Absolute Tempo" (No. 184).

Chapter 3

PEDAGOGY OF RHYTHM

A. General Materials and Combined Approaches

     This section contains materials which are general in nature or which present a combination of pedagogical approaches, and it should be used in conjunction with the following sections which concentrate on specific approaches. The literature offers a variety of helpful suggestions, procedures, and techniques for teaching rhythm based on the research and/ or teaching experience of the authors.

     Although they often contain a brief section on teaching rhythm, books on teaching school music are excluded. These should be investigated by the interested reader, as they occasionally throw a ray of light on certain aspects of the subject. A very small sampling of such literature includes the following:

Cheyette, Irving and Herbert Cheyette. Teaching Music
    Creatively in the Elementary School. New York:
    McGraw-Hill Book Co. , 1969.

Colwell, Richard J. The Teaching of Instrumental Music.
    New York: Appleton-Century-Crofts, Inc. , 1969.

Davison, Archibald T. Music Education in America. New
    York: Harper & Bros. , 1926.

Dykema, Peter W. and Hanna M. Cundiff. School Music
        Handbook. 2nd ed. Boston: C. C. Birchard &
        Co., 1955.

Gehrkens, Karl W. Music in the Grade Schools. Boston:
        C. C. Birchard & Co., 1934.

Holz, Emil A. and Roger E. Jacobi. Teaching Band Instru-
        ments to Beginners. Englewood Cliffs, NJ:
        Prentice-Hall, Inc., 1966.

Kohut, Daniel L. Instrumental Music Pedagogy: Teaching
        Techniques for School Band and Orchestra Directors.
        Englewood Cliffs, NJ: Prentice-Hall, Inc., 1973.

Mursell, James L. Music in American Schools. New York:
        Silver Burdett Co., 1943.

Nye, Robert E. and Vernice T. Nye. Music in the Elemen-
        tary School. 3rd ed. Englewood Cliffs, NJ:
        Prentice-Hall, Inc., 1970.

Raebeck, Lois and Lawrence Wheeler. New Approaches to
        Music in the Elementary School. 2nd ed. Dubuque,
        IA: William C. Brown Co., Inc., 1969.

For a somewhat dated but still useful annotated
bibliography of similar books which deal in part with teaching
rhythm, see No. 218, Marguerite V. Hood and E. J. Schultz,
Learning Music through Rhythm, pp. 175-78.

Selected adaptations of Orff and Kodály techniques
are included: see Bachmann (No. 189), Orff and Keetman
(No. 239), and Richards (No. 244). For some particularly
refreshing ways of developing rhythmic awareness, see R.
Murray Schafer's Ear Cleaning: ... (No. 249).

188. Atkinson, William C. Rhythm Lessons: A Course for
        Beginners in Bands and Orchestras. New York:
        Emil Ascher, Inc., 1928, 31 p.
        Briefly discusses rhythmic notation symbols and
terminology, meter signatures (including 5/4 and 7/4), tempo,

clapping and foot patting, and conducting patterns.   Short,
single-pitched musical examples are given.   The title is misleading, as the book is not designed for instrumentalists only;
it may be used by any beginning musician.

189.   Bachmann, Tibor.   Reading and Writing Music.   3 vols.
          Elizabethtown, PA: Continental Press, Inc. , 1968.
          The series consists of three volumes, teacher's
manuals and "liquid" duplicating masters of writing exercises
for each volume, and 200 Solfeggios: Supplementary Reading
Exercises.   The text is Bachmann's adaptation of Zoltan
Kodály's approach to teaching music in the elementary grades
by means of time-names, hand signals, tone games, pitch
syllables, dictation, and writing music.   The basic premise
of the series is that rhythmic understanding is essential to
music reading and must precede reading melodies with pitch
syllables.   The students first chant time-names, next asso-
ciate words with rhythm patterns, then play the patterns on
rhythm instruments, and finally write their own rhythm patterns.

190.   Baker, Martha.   "Counting and Rhythm." Clavier,
          IV/2 (Mar.-Apr. 1965) 20-21.
          A Dalcroze approach to teaching rhythm.   Also
suggests several mnemonic aids for counting rhythms and
ways to count basic subdivisions of the beat.

191.   Beeler, Walter.   "Things Are Seldom What They Seem."
          School Musician, XXXVII/7 (Mar. 1966) 64-65.
          States that rhythmic training should emphasize
eurhythmics more than mere arithmetic.   Deals primarily
with the inaccuracies and incompleteness inherent in printed
rhythms.

192.   Bell, Edith.   "Teaching Rhythm--A Symposium: IV.
          Follow the Stick!" Instrumentalist, XXIII/2 (Sept.
          1968) 73-75.
          Describes the author's approach to teaching basic
conducting patterns, rhythmic dictation, and durational values
of notes to elementary school children.

193.   Bolden, Joyce I.   The Influence of Selected Factors on
          Growth in Sight Singing and Rhythmic Reading.
          Ph.D. dissertation, Michigan State University, 1967,
          101 p. ; LC 67-14,475; DA XXVIII/6A, 2278.
          Investigates the influence of the piano keyboard,
syllables, letters, and the recorder on growth in sight singing

and rhythmic reading, and the effectiveness of each of these
modes of instruction as growth regulators. Rhythm syllables
were associated with eurhythmic feeling. It was found that
syllables and letters were most effective for developing rhythmic reading skill.

194.   Britton, Mervin W.   "A New Philosophy to Teaching
              Rhythm."   Percussionist, IX/2 (Winter 1971) 33-34.
        Based on material presented in the author's Rhythm in
Performance (No. 439).   Cites ten problems inherent in the whole
note (divisive) approach to teaching rhythms. Suggests teaching
beginning students the smallest practical rhythmic unit (sixteenth
note) first and then all new note values by addition. Also recommends using the word "count" to replace the word "beat."

195.   _____.   "Students Can Easily Read Rhythm--If."
              Instrumentalist, XXVI/11 (June 1972) 58-60.
        Discusses often misunderstood fundamentals of meter
signatures and rhythmic note relationships.

196.   Brody, Viola A.   "Certain Factors in Rhythm Training."
              Unpublished M. M. thesis, Eastman School of Music,
              University of Rochester, 1940, 87 p.
        An experimental study which determined the effective-
ness of a twenty-lesson rhythmic training course devised by the
author on the rhythmic coordination, recognition, and sight reading ability of ninety school children ranging from the fourth
through the twelfth grade. Results indicate that each rhythm factor requires a different ability and that improvement in one is
not necessarily associated with any appreciable improvement in
the others.

197.   Butler, Elizabeth W.   "Rhythmic Sequence, a Basis for
              Music Reading."   Unpublished M. M. Ed. thesis, Uni-
              versity of Michigan, 1946, 62 p.

198.   Campbell, Gail.   "Notation Using Rhythmic Patterns."
              Instrumentalist, XXV/2 (Sept. 1970) 89-90.
        Reports six conclusions of a study which identified
basic rhythmic patterns frequently performed incorrectly.

199.   Cheyette, Irving.   "On Teaching Rhythmic Reading."
              Educational Music Magazine, XXXIII (Nov. -Dec.
              1953) 23-24.
        Reasons that since rhythm must be felt muscularly,
and the tongue is a muscle, then verbalizing rhythmic patterns
is a good way to teach rhythm. The names of the months and

days and other words are used as mnemonic aids.

200. Chiuminatto, Anthony L.   "A Theory and Practice of
        Rhythmic Division."   Unpublished M. M. thesis,
        Northwestern University, 1941, 55 p.
        Advocates using the author's theory of "rhythmic
division" to teach rhythmic independence in the classroom.
Maintains that since the nature of music is one of melody
and accompaniment, rhythms should be taught by dividing the
class in half, assigning each half a slightly different rhythm,
and then performing the two rhythms simultaneously.

201. Cleeland, Joseph C.   "Psycho-Physiological Aspects
        of Rhythm as Applied to Vocal Pedagogy."   Unpub-
        lished M. M. thesis, Eastman School of Music,
        University of Rochester, 1931, 48 p.
        Considers the use of rhythm for training specific
groups of muscles which influence the production of vocal
tone, such as the muscles of breathing, phonation, resona-
tion, and articulation.

202. Coit, Lottie E.   Fun with Notes and Rests: A Basic
        Course in Rhythmic Development for Children in
        Elementary, Pre-Instrumental, and Piano Classes.
        Chicago: Clayton F. Summy Co. , 1943, 23 p.
        Includes teaching procedures, rhythm cards, and
piano music.   It is designed for use in the elementary grades,
pre-instrumental classes, general musicianship classes, and
rhythm band or orchestra.   Teaching units are graded so
that each note value (whole note through eighth note and corresponding rests) is presented one at a time.   Contains visual
aids for explaining note values and for understanding the nature of ensemble playing.

203. Colonna, Henry L.   "An Evaluation of Various Prac-
        tices and Devices Used in the Teaching of Rhythm
        in Elementary Music Education."   Unpublished M. S.
        thesis, Duquesne University, 1956, 60 p.
        Examines often confused concepts and definitions of
rhythm.   Evaluates the intrinsic worth and use of action songs,
dramatizations, singing games, folk dances, free rhythmic
activity with instrumental music, special rhythm instruments,
rhythm band, and toy orchestra to develop rhythm in children.

204. Cramer, William F.   "A Concept of Rhythm: Its Im-
        plications in Music Teaching Practice."   Unpublished
        M. A. thesis, Ohio State University, 1946, 60 p.

Evolves a philosophical concept of rhythm through
a survey of related historical, psychological, and philosophical literature, and the author's own observations and experiences. Suggests an approach to teaching rhythm whereby
the student abstracts an idea of rhythm after experiencing it
in many forms and combinations.

Dallin, Leon. Introduction to Music Reading: A Program for Personal Instruction. See No. 407.

205. Derick, Robert G. "A Method for Teaching of Music
       Reading through the Development of Rhythmic Under-
       standing." Unpublished M. M. thesis, University of
       Redlands, 1953.

206. De Yarman, Robert M. An Experimental Analysis of
       the Development of Rhythmic and Tonal Capabilities
       of Kindergarten and First Grade Children. Ph. D.
       dissertation, University of Iowa, 1971, 84 p. ;
       LC 71-30,424; DA XXXII/ 5A, 2727.
       The results of rhythmic aspects of this study indi-
cate that kindergarten and first grade children who received
varying amounts of instruction in "mixed" and "unusual"
meters generally performed criterion songs significantly better than their peers who received instruction in only "usual"
meters. Implications and results of this study are used
heavily by Edwin Gordon (De Yarman's dissertation advisor)
in The Psychology of Music Teaching (No. 98).

Dittemore, Edgar E. "An Investigation of Some Musical Capabilities of Elementary School Students." See No.
125.

207. Du Mont, Guilbert. "Some Causes of Error in Reading
       and Interpreting Rhythm." Unpublished M. S. thesis,
       University of Idaho, 1941, 21 p.
       Evaluates rhythmic instructional aspects of four
"standard" instrumental methods and seven class instrumental
methods. The sequence in which note values were presented
is discussed in relation to its effectiveness in developing muscular responses to rhythm. On the basis of the findings,
suggestions are made for music educators and writers of
method books.

208. Dyett, Walter H. "Development of Rhythm Mastery."
       Unpublished M. M. thesis, Chicago Musical College,
       Roosevelt University, 1942.

209.   Fairchild. Leslie.   "Solving Rhythmical Riddles."
          Etude, XLIV/10 (Oct. 1926) 719-20.
          Discusses the use of the metronome, primary and
secondary accents, and pulse subdivision.   Offers advice on
the performance of two against three, three against four,
tempo rubato, and multimeter.

          Feldman, Ivan W.   "The Rhythmic Approach to Band
Playing."   See No. 420.

210.   Fletcher, Stanley.   "Rhythm Is There Already."
          Piano Teacher, VI/5 (May-June 1964) 18-20.
          Urges music teachers to preserve the child's ca-
pacity for spontaneous enjoyment of rhythm by having him
participate in a musical context that is free from the mathematical difficulties of notation reading.   Suggests several
ostinato duets which may be used by the piano teacher for
this purpose.

211.   Francis, Ouida S.   "Swing Right, Swing Left."   Ameri-
          can Music Teacher, XVII/4 (Feb.-Mar. 1968) 29,
          43.
          Gives two suggestions for coping with rhythmic
problems, especially as they relate to piano performance:
swinging the body from side to side, and counting aloud say-
ing the names of the note values.   The latter activity is in-
completely explained.

          Gordon, Edwin.   The Psychology of Music Teaching.
See No. 98.

212.   Harris, Ernest E.   "Teaching Rhythm."   Music Edu-
          cation in Action.   Edited by Archie N. Jones.
          Boston: Allyn and Bacon, Inc., 1960, pp. 324-27.
          A valuable discussion on developing proper concepts
of perception and rendition of rhythmic patterns as groups of
notes.   Stresses teaching note values as felt relationships--
one to the other, and as they relate to the basic pulse.

213.   Hayes, Jane S.   "Teaching Rhythms through Song in the
          Elementary School."   Unpublished M.A. thesis,
          Ohio State University, 1956.   79 p.
          Decries the mathematical, mechanical, and drill ap-
proach to teaching rhythm.   States that if children gain a
"feeling" for fundamental rhythms through song and bodily
movement in the early elementary grades, they will be more
capable of learning and interpreting rhythmic notation in the

upper grades.   Criteria for evaluating songs to be used for
rhythmic experiences are listed.

214.   Helwig, Herman.   "Rhythmic Approach to Sight Read-
             ing."   Instrumentalist, IX/6 (Feb. 1955) 6-7.
       Suggests that rhythmic problems encountered during
a band rehearsal first be drilled on one note and then drilled
in context.

215.   Hix, Nelsie M.   "The Teaching of Rhythm in the Ele-
             mentary School."   Unpublished M.M. thesis,
             Illinois Wesleyan University, 1945, 132 p.
       Covers Dalcroze eurhythmics, theories for the ex-
perience of rhythm, metrical and phrase rhythms, teaching
aids, tests and measurements, and rhythmic exercises for
grades one through six.

216.   Holden, Florence S.   "The Evolution of Musical Rhythm
             and Methods of Teaching It in the Elementary
             School."   Unpublished M.M.Ed. thesis, Chicago
             Musical College, Roosevelt University, 1951, 96 p.
       An historical survey of rhythm from ancient to
modern times.   Outlines the philosophies and methods of
teaching rhythm of six well-known music educators in the
United States from 1900 to 1950.   Emphasizes the Jaques-
Dalcroze system of eurhythmics and its relation to music
education in the public schools.
       Includes a four-page introduction entitled "Rhythm
in Music" written by Karl W. Gehrkens which stresses artistic, flexible interpretation of rhythm.   Also includes a short,
annotated bibliography of materials dealing with primitive,
American Indian, and African rhythms, songs, and dances.

217.   Hood, Marguerite V.   Teaching Rhythm and Using
             Classroom Instruments.   Englewood Cliffs, NJ:
             Prentice-Hall, Inc., 1970, 142 p.
       Maintains that teaching rhythm in the elementary
school is made easier and more enjoyable for both the teacher
and children through the use of classroom instruments.
Part I, "Teaching Rhythm in the Elementary School," contains suggestions and procedures for teaching bodily movement to music and rhythm notation including rhythmic patterns,
word-chants, syncopation, time-names, "changing" and "unusual" meters.   Part II, "Using Classroom Instruments in
the General Music Program," offers chapters on traditional,
folk and national, tuned bar and keyboard, wind, and stringed
instruments.

The bibliographies, which include specialized books, elementary music series books, and recordings for each topic, are particularly valuable.

218. _____ and E. J. Schultz. <u>Learning Music through</u>
     <u>Rhythm</u>. Boston: Ginn & Co., 1949, 180 p.
     An excellent source book of rhythmic activities for grades one through six. One of its goals is "... to build <u>rhythm vocabularies for the ear and eye through physical</u> <u>activity</u>."--p. ix. Includes suggestions and 113 musical compositions for teaching rhythm and its notation. Pages 175-78 give an excellent, annotated bibliography of books containing material on rhythm.
     Review by William R. Sur in <u>Music Educators</u> <u>Journal</u>, XXXV/6 (May-June 1949) 45.

219. Hounchell, Robert F. "A Comprehensive Outline for
     the Teaching of Rhythmic Reading." <u>Percussionist</u>,
     V/4 (May 1968) 338-48; VI/1 (Oct. 1968) 24-29.
     Accurate rhythmic responses to notated patterns
     (termed 'sounds') are a result of conditioning by
     means of the systematic experiencing of such re-
     sponses. Instantaneous responses are developed
     through a set of comprehensive lessons consisting
     of duple, triple, and syncopated patterns set in
     duple and triple meters. The student's response
     to these involves his 'syllabification' of the
     'sounds' while beating or conducting the meter....
     --<u>RILM Abstracts</u>, II/2 (May-Aug. 1968) 204.

     Houseknecht, Bruce H. "A Course of Study for the
Junior High School Band." See No. 423.

220. Isaac, Merle J. "Teaching Rhythm." <u>Instrumentalist</u>,
     XXI/1 (Aug. 1966) 47.
     Gives ten suggestions for teaching rhythm to string
players.

221. Jenkins, Ella L. <u>This Is Rhythm</u>. New York: Oak
     Publications, Inc., 1962, 96 p.
     Explores simple uses of rhythm and song through
the employment of percussion instruments and body movement. The book is designed especially for the blind, the
deaf, the mentally retarded, and the emotionally disturbed
child.
     Review in <u>Music Educators Journal</u>, XLIX/1 (Sept.-
Oct. 1962) 128.

222.   Jones, Archie N.   "Rhythmic Awareness."   <u>Educational</u>
       <u>Music Magazine</u>, XXXV (Jan.-Feb. 1956) 45-46.
       Lists forty-five techniques for making pupils aware
of rhythm.

223.   Kessinger, Newell L.   "An Analysis of Errors in In-
       strumental Sight Reading."   Unpublished M.S. the-
       sis, Illinois State Normal University, 1950.

224.   Kinscella, Hazel G.   "Teaching Rhythm in Class Les-
       sons."   <u>Etude</u>, XL/1 (Jan. 1922) 10.
       Suggests some musical games which develop rhyth-
mic feeling.   Designed for use in piano class lessons.

225.   Kitchen, Alice F.   "Rhythm: Its Place and Importance
       in Group Teaching."   <u>Clavier</u>, II/1 (Jan.-Feb.
       1963) 37-41.
       Discusses counting simple rhythms and the use of
rhythmic movement.   Five suggestions are made for group
rhythmic activities.

226.   Lauritzen, Adrian R.   "Some Psychophysical Implica-
       tions of Rhythm Pedagogy in the Primary Grades."
       Unpublished D. Mus. Ed. dissertation, Chicago Mu-
       sical College, Roosevelt University, 1954, 113 p.
       Discusses
           ... six areas of research: (1) a brief historical
           background of some psychological studies of
           rhythm;   (2) a survey of some concepts of
           rhythm;   (3) a brief historical review of the
           pedagogical approach to rhythm in the schools
           of the United States from the time of Lowell
           Mason to the present day;   (4) rhythmic skills
           as related to child growth and development;
           (5) the role of the classroom teacher;   and
           (6) a review of some of the psychophysical im-
           plications of rhythm pedagogy in the primary
           grades. --pp. 8-9.
       Considers four benefits resulting from musical
stimuli and rhythmic response: the pleasure derived, the
relief from tension, the improvement of bodily posture, and
the resultant contribution to the creative impulse.

227.   Laycock, Ralph.   "Introducing Contemporary Rhythms."
       <u>Instrumentalist</u>, XXIII/7 (Feb. 1969) 73-74; XXIII/8
       (Mar. 1969) 70-73;   XXIII/9 (Apr. 1969) 80-83.
       Contains exercises to develop a natural feeling for

"asymmetric" rhythms, exercises designed for specific compositions, and exercises which use multimeter.   Stresses
conducting and teaching techniques for the school music director.

228.   Leimer, Karl.   Rhythmics, Dynamics, Pedal and Other
          Problems of Piano Playing.   Translated by Frederick
          C. Rauser.   Philadelphia: Theodore Presser Co. ,
          1938, 64 p.
          Chapter III, "Rhythmics," applicable to all instru-
mentalists, contains somewhat dated discussions of definitions
of rhythm;   notation of duplets, triplets, and quadruplets;   the
"up-beat";   syncopation;   and tempo.   Offers pedagogical procedures for counting rhythms.

229.   McKenzie, Jack.   "Some Performance Problems of Con-
          temporary Percussion Composition. "   Percussionist,
          II/4 (Sept. 1965) 1-6.
          Presents examples of and points out performance
problems in the compositions of Benjamin Johnston and
Michael Colgrass which use metric modulation, micro-rhyth-
mic notation, and odd-rhythmic groupings.   Suggests a for-
mula to use in performing odd rhythmic groupings which has
been used successfully by the author with students as young
as junior high school age.

230.   Magnell, Elmer.   "Teaching Rhythm--A Symposium:
          III. Systems for Reading Rhythm at Sight. "   In-
          strumentalist, XXIII/2 (Sept. 1968) 68-70.
          Makes general observations on the importance of
rhythm in sight reading and surveys the following eight approaches to rhythmic training: 1) "Counting, Chanting,
Clapping, Conducting";   2) use of the "and" principle;   3) the
"down-up" principle;   4) the "pendulum swing" principle;
5) the "time-unit" principle;   6) the "clock-orientation" principle described by Adela Bay in "The Time Problem" (see
No. 367);   7) the "word-chanting" principle;   and 8) tachistoscopic techniques.   Little is said about the merits or demerits
of any of the approaches.

       Mainwaring, James.   "Psychological Factors in the
Teaching of Music. "   See No. 142.

231.   Maiocco, Dominick O.   Do You Skip Beats?   Phoenix,
          AZ: By the Author, 4743 N. 58th Drive, 1957,
          7 p.
          Suggests four exercises to help musicians who have

difficulty sustaining meter: use of aural imagination, tapping
the foot on the first and third counts in 4/4 meter (not often
mentioned in other texts), counting according to phrase structure, and alternating left and right foot taps for fast tempi.

Matthay, Tobias. <u>Musical Interpretation: Its Laws
and Principles, and Their Application in Teaching and Performing.</u> See No. 23.

232.   Milak, John.   "An Application of Certain Learning
        Theories to the Teaching of Musical Rhythm."
        <u>Missouri Journal of Research in Music Education,</u>
        II/3 (Autumn 1969) 49-67.
        The purpose of this study
            ... is to examine and apply certain basic types
            of learning to certain aspects of music education
            and to build and test a sequence of instruction
            upon ideas and concepts derived from these types
            of learning. --<u>Musical Article Guide,</u> V/1 (Winter
            1969-1970) 32.

233.   Monsour, Sally;   Marilyn C. Cohen;   and Patricia E.
        Lindell.   <u>Rhythm in Music and Dance for Children.</u>
        Belmont, CA: Wadsworth Publishing Co. , 1966,
        99 p.
            This book contains a variety of approaches,
            teaching media, materials, and activities to en-
            able teachers of various backgrounds, as well as
            physical education and music specialists, to con-
            duct lessons in rhythm, using music and dance,
            for children in the first eight grades. --Preface.
        Included are general references for rhythms and
creative movement, music and dance collections, costume,
poetry, films, art prints, rhythmic records for general use,
recordings for singing games and folk dances.   Page 38 offers a collection of mnemonic aids for teaching five basic
rhythm patterns.

234.   Moore, E. C.   <u>Playing at Sight.</u>   Kenosha, WI:
        G. Leblanc Co. , 1953, 35 p.
        The section on "counting time," pp. 9-10, explains
and diagrams the author's system of counting rhythms.   Suggests feeling rhythms kinesthetically by means of the foot tap
and by counting aloud.   Comments on the importance of a
counting system for developing sight reading skill.

235.   Moorhead, Gladys E. and Donald Pond.   <u>Music of</u>

Young Children. Part I: Chant, 1941, 23 p. ;
Part II: General Observations, 1942, 36 p. ;
Part III: Musical Notation, 1944, 25 p. Santa
Barbara, CA: Pillsbury Foundation for Advance-
ment of Music Education.
  A study which observes children at the Pillsbury
Foundation School who were allowed to move, sing, and use
instruments and sound-producing devices in an unrestricted
manner. Investigates rhythm patterns in chant sung by these
children, examines rhythmic cells characteristic of their instrumental music, and reports on the method in which they
were taught to read and write rhythmic notation. States that
activities such as rhythm band restrict and inhibit the child's
own rhythmic flow; each child should be free to feel and experience rhythm in his own way.

236. Mouton, Jerome. "Mambo Rhythms." Instrumentalist,
      XXIV/2 (Sept. 1969) 73-74, 79-81.
  Discusses the importance of understanding mambo
rhythms for the concert or stage band director. Suggests
typical mambo rhythmic patterns for the bongos, congas,
timbales, cencerro, and claves.

237. Mowery, Richard R. "Concepts in Rhythm Teaching
      and Reading." Unpublished M. M. Ed. thesis, Drake
      University, 1953, 46 p.
  Discusses the history, definition, and methods of
teaching rhythm. Suggestions are given for mastering rhythms
by writing and practicing them on a single pitch. The author's technique for teaching new rhythmic patterns one measure or less in length is to construct a three-measure phrase
in which the first measure sets the pulse, the second presents the new pattern, and the third uses it in context.

238. Mursell, James L. "Some Basic Principles in the
      Teaching of Rhythm." Yearbook of the Music
      Supervisors National Conference, (1929) 529-36.
  Discusses rhythm as the common foundation of musical technique and expression. Deplores teaching rhythm as
though it was a system of fixed mathematical relationships.
"We have not taught, and the pupil has not learned, rhythm
until it has been sensed intimately and inwardly in terms of
muscular action and co-ordination."--p. 533.

239. Orff, Carl and Gunild Keetman. Orff-Schulwerk,
      Music for Children. Vol. I: Pentatonic. English
      adaptation by Doreen Hall and Arnold Walter.

Mainz: B. Schott's Söhne, 1956, 95 p.
Orff's starting point is rhythm.... It is not
taught mechanically, mathematically (by subdivisions of whole notes perhaps or by counting
beats) it grows out of speech-patterns. For the
child ... music and movement are an indivisible
entity; it is this intimate connection, which leads
quite naturally from speech-patterns to rhythm,
from rhythmical patterns to melody. Speech-
patterns make it possible for a child to grasp
every type of meter without difficulty, even up-
beats or irregular bars. Rhythmical formulas
so experienced are reproduced by clapping,
stamping, body-slapping; and, later, on percussion instruments which provide accompaniments
of steadily increasing complexity. --Introduction
to Vol. I.
Of special interest are the numerous common word
phrases set to rhythms in the section entitled "Studies in
Rhythm and Melody, A. Speech-Patterns," pp. 66-70 and
"B. Ostinati," pp. 71-78.
See also Vol. II: <u>Major: Bordun</u>, 1960, 48 p.;
Vol. III: <u>Major: Triads</u>, 1960, 40 p.; Vol. IV: <u>Minor:
Bordun</u>, 1961, 40 p.; Vol. V: <u>Minor: Triads</u>, 1961, 39 p.;
and <u>Teacher's Manual</u>, 1960, 40 p.

240.   Perfield, Effa E. "Exercise for Developing Rhythm
       and Note Values without Fractional Reasoning."
       <u>Musician</u>, XXII/2 (Feb. 1917) 94; XXII/4 (Apr.
       1917) 252-53.
       Describes teaching note values to young children by
means of kinesthesis and elementary mathematical puzzle-
stories.

241.   Pottenger, Harold P. <u>An Analysis of Rhythm Reading
       Skill</u>. D. Mus. Ed. dissertation, Indiana University,
       1969, 402 p.; LC 69-16,643; DA XXX/4A, 1590-
       91.
       Determines relationships among rhythm reading
skill and certain abilities and factors which are requisite or
desirable components or concomitants of that skill, and offers
recommendations for training and research in music reading.
A battery of tests was administered to instrumentalists on
levels from elementary school to college. One interesting
recommendation suggested by findings of the study was that
emphasis in both training and research should be given in attention to perceptual and conceptual aspects of rhythm reading

skill, especially to aural imagery and cognition of note-rest relative values and beat values.

242. Rabanal, John A. "Teaching Rhythm to Instrumental
        Students in the Upper Elementary Grades." Unpub-
        lished M. M. Ed. thesis, Drake University, 1955,
        28 p.
        Evaluates methods and procedures used by the au-
thor to teach rhythm to elementary school instrumentalists.
Examines the correlation of academic grades, Iowa Tests of
Basic Skills scores, and Kwalwasser Music Talent Test
scores to pupil musicianship.

243. Richards, Mary H. "The Legacy from Kodály."
        Music Educators Journal, XLIX/ 6 (June-July 1963)
        27-30.
        An account of the Kodály system as adapted by the
author for use in the Portola Valley Public Schools in California.

244. _____. Threshold to Music. Palo Alto, CA:
        Fearon Publishers, Inc. , 1964, 142 p.
        Includes 118 Experience Charts bound in one volume.
Presents an approach to teaching music in the first three elementary grades using the author's adaptation of the educational
principles and philosophy of Zoltan Kodály. Stresses reading
and feeling rhythmic pulse and rhythmic patterns. Incorpor-
ates a system of rhythm syllables similar to the French time-
names. Sets of illustrated "Experience Charts" are available
for each grade, but the poor quality of music notation would
tend to teach the students subliminally non-standard notation
at their most impressionable age. "Some of the rhythmic
ideas that are found in Threshold to Music may be traced to
the influence of Carl Orff."--Preface, p. xi.
        The Fourth Year: Teacher's Manual, Including Ex-
perience Charts (Palo Alto, CA: Fearon Publishers, Inc. ,
1967, 28 p.) is a continuation of Threshold to Music.
        See also Mary H. Richards, "The Kodály System in
the Elementary Schools," Council for Research in Music Education Bulletin, No. 8 (Fall 1966) 44-48.

245. Rickaby, T. L. "Irregular Rhythms." Etude,
        XXXVIII/1 (Jan. 1920) 8.
        A commentary, reflecting the attitude of some mu-
sicians at the time, which states that "musical riddles" such
as 5/4 and 7/4 meter, changing meters, and the "two against
three rhythm" may be left out of ordinary courses in music.

These tasks can be undertaken only by the elect.
They cannot be taught to anyone.   Players either
can do them or they cannot.   So, while developing rhythmic perception and feeling as much as
possible, do not waste time on difficulties that
are of doubtful benefit even where there is a pos-
sibility of their being well done, for this possi-
bility is frequently a slippery and elusive quan-
tity.

246.   Roop, Edyth W.   "Rhythm: Basic Element in Music as
       in Life."   Clavier, VI/9 (Dec. 1967) 28-31.
       Suggests a rhythmically oriented outline for teaching
and learning a new composition.

247.   Rosenblum, Sandra P.   "Rhythm and Fingering--A His-
       torical Survey."   Piano Teacher, VII/4 (Mar.-Apr.
       1965) 12-14.
       A collection of hints, suggestions, and admonitions
concerning rhythm and counting by ten authors of keyboard
and violin tutors written during the 17th, 18th, and 19th centuries.

248.   Schaefer, Jay D.   "The Teaching of Rhythms to the
       Beginner."   Instrumentalist, XXI/6 (Jan. 1967)
       36-37.
       Discusses advantages to be gained by introducing
quarter, eighth, and sixteenth notes immediately after the
student has started to play the whole note correctly.

249.   Schafer, R. Murray.   Ear Cleaning: Notes for an Ex-
       perimental Music Course.   Don Mills, Ont.: BMI
       Canada Ltd., 1967, 46 p.
       Included for its brief but creative discussion of
rhythm (lecture eight).   Contains a list of suggested exercises, discussions, and assignments designed to stimulate
class discussion and participation in rhythmic experiences.
       Review by Peter Dickinson in Music in Education,
XXXII/332 (July-Aug. 1968) 202; Karl Kroeger in Notes,
XXVI/1 (Sept. 1969) 50-51.

250.   Schaum, John W.   Rhythm Speller.   Melville, NY:
       Belwin Mills Publishing Corp., 1950, 32 p.
       This is a workbook which attempts to provide the
student with a mental grasp of rhythmic construction.   It is
intended to be used as soon as the student learns fractions
in his school arithmetic class.   By means of explanatory

charts, diagrams, and quizzes (the answers to which are provided for the teacher), the book aims to give the student an
understanding of the durational values of notes and rests so
that he might comprehend the mechanics of rhythm, counting,
and measure construction. No attempt is made to teach the
feeling of rhythm.

251. Schelhas, Evelyn V. "Rhythm and Rhyme 'Round the
       Year." Educational Music Magazine, XXXV (Sept. -
       Oct. 1955) 29a-44a; XXXV (Nov.-Dec. 1955) 25b-
       40b; XXXV (Jan.-Feb. 1956) 25c-40c; XXXV
       (Mar.-Apr. 1956) 27d-38d.
       Includes suggestions and music (associated with the
seasons of the year) for teaching children basic rhythmic
movement and rhythm instruments.

252. Schwadron, Abraham A. "Teaching Odd Meters: An
       Exemplary Approach." Instrumentalist, XXVI/5
       (Dec. 1971) 26-29.
       Discusses the need for and an approach to the prep-
aration of pedagogical materials for teaching "odd" meters.
Particularly valuable for its excellent suggestions, guidelines,
and organization of materials. Includes one page of examples
entitled "Odd Rhythms for Clarinet."

253. Seagondollar, Owen W. "The Rhythmic Unit Content of
       Three Vocal Primers, Three Band Primers, and
       Three Orchestra Primers." Unpublished M.A. the-
       sis, Colorado State College, 1942, 50 p.
       Discusses rhythmic patterns which are found in the
primers and indicates by means of a frequency table their
relative importance so that an instructor may know what
rhythms should be emphasized in his teaching program. The
small sample investigated places a limited value on the conclusions of this research.

254. Sehon, Elizabeth and Emma Lou O'Brien. Rhythms in
       Elementary Education. New York: Ronald Press
       Co. , 1951, 247 p.
       A text for the elementary teacher containing a wide
variety of techniques and materials. Discusses the educational objectives of rhythm in education; creativity in rhythmic movement; its musical accompaniment; general needs;
characteristics, and interests of children; outlines and suggestions for rhythmic activities; activity songs, verses,
poems, and nursery rhymes; rhythmic patterns of words,
phrases, verses, and poems; folk singing, games, and

dances;   culminations of rhythmic activities;   and philosophy,
child guidance, materials, bibliographies, class organization,
and evaluation for the teacher.

The appendix suggests sample theme lessons;   projects based on principles of time, force, and space;   activity
songs, poems, rhymes, and singing games;   and contains a
five-page bibliography of music, recordings, and books.

255.   Shlimovitz, H. M.   The Rhythm Singer.   Melville,
          NY: Belwin Mills Publishing Corp. , 1957, 16 p.
Attempts to teach rhythm to youngsters by having
them sing thirty-eight well known melodies while reading the
rhythms of the songs notated on one pitch on the staff.   The
foreword suggests that the student should use bodily movement and percussion instruments to accompany the songs but
offers no further instruction in this regard.   A chart of "time
values" is included but not related to the songs in any way.

256.   Skornicka, Joseph E.   The Function of Time and
          Rhythm in Instrumental Music Reading Competency.
          Ed.D. dissertation, Oregon State College, 1958,
          76 p. ;   LC 58-3059;   DA XIX/6A, 1406-7.
          An experiment was conducted to determine whether
          an early and constant emphasis on time and
          rhythm would significantly improve instrumental
          music reading.   A control group of 72 elementary
          students was equated with an experimental group
          of 77 elementary students by means of the Drake
          Musical Aptitude Test.   Each of five teachers
          taught both a control ... sub-group and an exper-
          imental sub-group.   The experimental groups
          used materials which were especially adapted to
          the counting of time and recognition of rhythm
          patterns.   The control groups were taught by the
          conventional method used by the participating
          teachers.   The investigator constructed and ad-
          ministered two music reading tests.   The first
          was administered at the beginning of the experi-
          mental period, the second at the middle of the
          experimental period. ...   The method of instruc-
          tion that emphasized time and rhythm in early
          training developed more competent music reading
          than methods that did not provide this emphasis.
          Emphasis on time and rhythm which combined the
          tonguing and playing of quarter notes and rests
          as the initial units of time as well as the tapping
          of the foot and playing on the march as the

physical response to the beat, appeared to develop
a stronger feeling for the beat and produced more
competent instrumental music reading than the
method which did not include these procedures in
training. --Erwin H. Schneider and Henry L. Cady,
Evaluation and Synthesis of Research Studies ... ,
pp. 447-48.

Quarter notes were introduced to the experimental
group as soon as each student could hold a tone in the easy
range of his instrument for ten seconds. Half, dotted-half,
and whole notes were introduced later. The control group
began their training in the traditional manner, with whole
notes and whole rests. This was followed by the introduction
of half and quarter notes and rests, in that order. On page
35 of the dissertation, Skornicka states that

It will be noted that the order of the introduction
of whole, half and quarter notes and rests was
exactly reversed in the experimental and control
groups. Therefore, the difference in the training of the two groups was found in the sequence
of presentation of musical notation which formed
the basis for procedures that made emphasis on
time and rhythm possible.

This has led Alan H. Drake in his review of this
dissertation to deduce that the Boosey & Hawkes Band Method
by Skornicka and Bergeim was used for the experimental
method. Drake comments that "The use of the quarter note
seems such a logical way to proceed that this reviewer is
surprised that twenty-four years after the publication of the
Boosey and Hawkes Band Method, no other major method
book has utilized the same approach."--p. 45.

Review by Alan H. Drake in Council for Research
in Music Education Bulletin, No. 27 (Winter 1972) 44-46.

See also No. 435, Joseph E. Skornicka, Boosey &
Hawkes Instrumental Course.

257.   Slider, Robert. "Teaching Basic Rhythm." Instru-
          mentalist, XIII/7 (Mar. 1959) 95-96.
          An account of the author's procedure for teaching
rhythm.

258.   Sloane, Helen S. "Why Rhythms?" Educational Music
          Magazine, XXXIII (Nov.-Dec. 1953) 16-17.
          Presents some social and musical values of teaching
rhythm to children.

259.   Smith, Eula M. "Devices for Teaching Musical
          Rhythms in the Elementary School." Unpublished

M. A. thesis, Ball State Teachers College, 1951,
111 p.
Briefly surveys problems involved in rhythmic training on the elementary level. Describes the nature of rhythm
and outlines its evolution from ancient times to the 20th century. Techniques for teaching rhythm are presented in three
classifications: kinesthetic or muscular response in various
types of movement; mnemonic devices, methods of counting,
and syllabification of rhythms; and instrumental devices, including rhythm band. Suggests a possible sequence for the
study of rhythm for grades one through six utilizing rhythmic
movement, reading activities, and instrumental activities.

260.   Smith, Frances E.   "The Use of Rhythms in the Ele-
            mentary School. " Unpublished M. M. thesis, North-
            western University, 1949, 66 p.
Discusses old and new concepts of teaching rhythm,
definitions, bodily response to rhythm, uses of rhythm instruments. Suggests certain types of rhythmic experiences for
children from kindergarten to sixth grade. An annotated
bibliography of books and recordings for experiencing rhythm
through dramatizations, games, and dances is appended.

261.   Smolin, Harry (ed.).   Xavier Cugat's Latin-American
            Rhythms for Pianists, Accordionists, Arrangers.
            New York: Robbins Music Corp. , 1941, 40 p.
Contains brief text describing the rhythmic interpretation of the rumba, tango, conga, and samba, and gives
examples of typical piano and accordion accompaniments in
various styles to well-known melodies for each of these four
dance rhythms.

262.   Talley, Howard.   "The Cross-Rhythm Problem. "
            Clavier, II/ 3 (May-June 1963) 20.
Suggests two methods for teaching the "three-against-
two rhythm. " The musical example used to illustrate the
rhythm is notated incorrectly.

263.   Tobias, Sister M.   "Teaching Rhythm in the Primary
            Grades. " Musart, XVII/ 5 (Apr. -May 1965) 46-49.
A general discussion touching on the use of movement, songs, mnemonics, and rhythm band. The task of the
teacher, according to the author, is to develop the child's
rhythmic capacity so that he will listen to rhythm, feel it
correctly, and relate these skills to printed music.

264.   Tongg, Geraldine.   "Teaching Rhythm in the Elementary

School." Unpublished M. M. Ed. thesis, University
of Michigan, 1958, 77 p.

265.   Tucker, Gerald L.   The Influence of Isolated Rhythmic
       Drill on Growth in Sight Singing.   D. Mus. Ed. dis-
       sertation, University of Oklahoma, 1969, 154 p. ;
       LC 70-2342;   DA XXX/8A, 3497.
          Fifteen college students were used as experimental
subjects and were presented with the rhythmic portion of a
unit of study in sight singing until the midpoint of the experimental semester, at which time the harmonic and melodic
portions of the unit of study were presented.   An equal number of control group subjects dealt with all the elements of
sight singing concurrently.   Neither group's progress was
significantly better than the other's in terms of overall performance.

266.   Vanasek, Benedict.   Student's Manual of Music Rhythms:
       Including a Modern Music Vocabulary; Questions
       and Answers for Vocal and Instrumental Students.
       New York: Mills Music Inc. , 1938, 20 p.

267.   VanderCook, H. A.   Expression in Music.   Rev. ed.
       Chicago: Rubank, Inc. , 1942, 57 p.
          First written in 1926, this useful handbook examines
some common faults of poor stylistic and expressive musical
performance and suggests detailed remedies for their correction.   Especially applicable are the chapters on dotted
rhythms, syncopation, tied and slurred notes, and the performance of staccato.   The proper control of the factors of
tone quality, volume, and especially duration form the basis
for most of the principles of expression mentioned.   The text
is supported by fifty-seven musical examples.

268.   Van Patten, Leroy.   Revised Standard Notation of
       TIME in Music.   Rev. ed.   Glens Falls, NY:
       By the Author, 61 Broad St. , 1969, 36 p.
          An intentionally polemic disquisition on the teaching
of "time" to beginning music students.   Cites inconsistencies
in durational notation and terminology as presently used and
suggests specific revisions for their improvement.

269.   Vanskike, Howard and Clay Bellew.   Rhythm-Reading-
       Readiness.   St. Louis, MO: Van-Lew Publishing
       Co. , 1951, 39 p.
          The authors have attempted to isolate the problem
       of the teaching of rhythm on the ground that it is

an academic problem; not music but an element employed in music. Patterns used in the text are in music notation simply because music notation if familiar. Analysis and 'activation' of all rhythmic patterns constitute the main portion of the book, with explanatory notes for the teacher and the student and a foreword by Mark Hindsley. It is not recommended for any particular grade level but is designed to help meet and solve the problem of basic rhythmic training wherever the need is encountered.... --from review in Instrumentalist, VI/5 (Mar.-Apr. 1952) 4, 41.

270.   Verhaalen, Sister Marion. "Formalizing Creative Rhythmic Experiences." Musart, XX/1 (Sept.-Oct. 1967) 14-15, 31-32.
Suggests that rhythmic notation should be presented to elementary school children as soon as they have experienced free, creative rhythmic movement. Notational symbols should be presented with their correct names and should be chanted against a steady recurring pulsation.

271.   Vincent, John N., Jr. "A Study of Devices Used in Teaching Musical Rhythm." Unpublished M.A. thesis, George Peabody College for Teachers, 1933.

272.   Walter, Arnold. "Carl Orff's 'Music for Children'." Instrumentalist, XIII/5 (Jan. 1959) 38-39.
An authoritative explanation of Orff's pedagogical approach.

273.   Whitnall, Faith. "The Rhythmic Objectives of a College Preparatory Program." Unpublished M.M. Ed. thesis, University of Michigan, 1944, 81 p.

274.   Wilson, F. "Improve Our Bands by Teaching Rhythm." School Musician, XXXVIII (Nov. 1966) 60-61.

275.   Withers, Tom R. "Rhythm in Music Education." Unpublished M.M. thesis, Northwestern University, 1949.

276.   Wourinen, Charles. "Notes on the Performance of Contemporary Music." Perspectives of New Music, III/1 (Fall-Winter 1964) 10-21.
Suggests that difficulty in reading and performing complex rhythmic patterns is not inherent but rather cultural

in origin and due to habits acquired by most players in their training.   Recommends a way for the performer to learn to execute the "irrational" rhythms of contemporary music.

Zimmerman, Marilyn P.   Musical Characteristics of Children.   See No. 117.

B.   Eurhythmics and Rhythmic Movement

Some form of rhythmic movement is widely acknowledged to be inherent in most musical activities, at least in their basic stages.   The Jaques-Dalcroze system of eurhythmics exerted a strong influence on music education in the first half of the 20th century (see Boepple [Nos. 281 and 282], Gehrkens [No. 294], Glenn [No. 296], MSNC Research Council [No. 314], and Schuster [No. 322]) and gradually became incorporated into its mainstream.   As Rupert Thackray notes in his review of Jaques-Dalcroze's Rhythm, Music and Education (see No. 306), it is interesting that Carl Orff "... taught on Dalcroze's methods at the Günter Schule in Munich from 1925 to 1936, the period during which his Schulwerk was published."   In much less formalized ways, rhythmic movement and eurhythmics still underlie the fundamental philosophy of numerous approaches to teaching rhythm, some of which employ the foot tap, hand clap, and other body motions.   Materials on these techniques are included in Section D.   Miscellaneous Approaches (Nos. 364-405).

The literature listed in this category contains descriptive material and teaching procedures.   With a few exceptions, books consisting mostly of song collections or musical accompaniments for rhythmic activities are not included.   Those who want a comprehensive, annotated listing of these will find one in the bibliography of Monsour, Cohen, and Lindell's Rhythm in Music and Dance for Children (No. 233)

under the section entitled "Music and Dance Collections,"
pp. 89-90.

See also writings related to this subject such as
those dealing with motor rhythm and kinesthesis in the first
three sections of Chapter 2.

277.   Andrews, Gladys.   Creative Rhythmic Movement for
       Children.   Englewood Cliffs, NJ: Prentice-Hall,
       Inc. , 1954, 198 p.
           Based on the author's doctoral dissertation (see
No. 278).   Discusses periods of child development and sug-
gests creative rhythmic activities and teaching procedures.
Contains sixty-six simple piano accompaniments for songs
and dances and many illustrations.
           Review in Etude, LXXIII/7 (July 1955) 6;   Music
Educators Journal, XLI/1 (Sept. -Oct. 1954) 20.

278.   _____.   A Study to Describe and Relate Experiences
       for the Use of Teachers Interested in Guiding Crea-
       tive Rhythmic Movement.   Ed. D. dissertation, New
       York University, 1952, 351 p. ;   LC A53-150;   DA
       XIII/1, 33.
           Examines the needs and characteristics of children
in early and middle childhood and deals with the nature of
creative rhythmic movement.   Contains a manual concerned
with the contributions of creative rhythmic expression to the
development of children in the elementary school.

279.   _____ and Marion Bozenhard.   "Suggestions for a
       Course of Study in Creative Rhythms for Children."
       Unpublished M. S. thesis, University of Wisconsin,
       1939.

280.   Belcher, Beverly J.   "Begin Piano with Rhythm."
       Music Journal, XXVII/4 (Apr. 1969) 75.
           Brief remarks on bodily movement as an aid to
mastering rhythm problems.

281.   Boepple, Paul.   "Demonstration of Dalcroze Euryth-
       mics."   Yearbook of the Music Supervisors National
       Conference, (1931) 306-7.
           Deals with the stress Dalcroze places upon providing
musical instruction through actual experience rather than
through theoretical knowledge.

282. _____. "The Study of Rhythm." Yearbook of the
        Music Supervisors National Conference, (1931) 192-
        94.
        A brief discussion of Dalcroze eurhythmics, em-
phasizing its physiological aspects, by the director of the
American Dalcroze Institute in New York City.

283. Boyle, John D. The Effect of Prescribed Rhythmical
        Movements on the Ability to Sight Read Music.
        Ph. D. dissertation, University of Kansas, 1968,
        195 p.; LC 68-17,359: DA XXIX/7A, 2290-91.
        Concludes that a program of rhythmic training in-
corporating bodily movement in the form of foot tapping to
mark the underlying beat and hand clapping to practice
rhythm patterns enables junior high school bandsmen to score
significantly higher on a rhythm sight reading test and the
Watkins-Farnum Performance Scale than bandsmen who did
not receive training employing bodily movement.

284. _____. "The Effect of Prescribed Rhythmical Move-
        ments on the Ability to Read Music at Sight."
        Journal of Research in Music Education, XVIII/4
        (Winter 1970) 307-18.
        Based on the author's doctoral dissertation (see No.
283).

285. _____. "Rhythm Sight Reading: The Key to Music
        Sight Reading." Instrumentalist, XXIV/2 (Sept.
        1969) 42-43.
        A synopsis of the author's doctoral dissertation
(see No. 283).

286. Brown, Lillian W. Studies in Basic Rhythms for
        Young Children. Cincinnati, OH: Willis Music
        Co., 1956.

287. Christiansen, Helen M. Bodily Rhythmic Movements
        of Young Children in Relation to Rhythm in Music:
        An Analytical Study of an Organized Curriculum in
        Bodily Rhythms, Including Potential and Functioning
        Aspects in Selected Nursery School, Kindergarten
        and First Grade Groups. Ph. D. dissertation,
        Bureau of Publications, Teachers College, Columbia
        University, 1938, 196 p.
        Declares that bodily rhythms, taught as an integral
part of the day's activities, are a source of growth and enjoyment to every child regardless of his mental capacity or
special abilities.

288.   Doll, Edna and Mary J. Nelson.   Rhythms Today!
       Morristown, NJ: Silver Burdett Co. , 1965,
       197 p.
       A handbook for starting and developing a program
of creative movement with children from pre-school through
the upper elementary grades.   Contains procedures, games,
and activities to develop children's physical responses to
rhythm and sound.   Recordings are available to accompany
the lessons in the book.
       Review by Adeline McCall in Music Educators
Journal, LII/1 (Sept. -Oct. 1965) 140-41.

289.   Driver, Ann.   Music and Movement.   London: Oxford
       University Press, 1936, 122 p.
       A classic book in the field, still in wide use.   Its
main thesis is that movement is the natural foundation for a
sound musical education.   Contains a unique discussion of music and movement for boys.

290.   Driver, Ethel.   A Pathway to Dalcroze Eurhythmics.
       London: Thomas Nelson & Sons, 1951, 102 p.
       A helpful guidebook containing suggestions and les-
son plans for teaching eurhythmics to classes and individuals.
Includes eighty musical excerpts.
       Review in Musical Opinion, LXXV/891 (Dec. 1951)
157.

291.   Fardig, Sheldon P.   Effect of a Kinesthetic-Rhythm
       Activity to Music on Selected Aspects of Behavior.
       Ph. D. dissertation, Northwestern University, 1966,
       225 p. ;   LC 67-4219; DA XXVII/12A, 4279.
       Examines the effect of a group experience in rhyth-
mic bodily movement to music upon personality characteristics, creativity responses, self-concept expression, rhythmic
discrimination ability, and interest in music.   Findings indicate that propositions concerning the salutary effects of rhythmic movement should be looked upon with some reserve.

292.   Findlay, Elsa.   Rhythm and Movement: Applications of
       Dalcroze Eurhythmics.   Evanston, IL: Summy-
       Birchard Co. , 1971, 89 p.
              A beautiful and very practical presentation in
       which Dalcroze Eurhythmics are applied.   Pri-
       mary and elementary teachers of music and/or
       dance will find the book invaluable.   Illustrations,
       charts and well-written, very appropriate music
       scores are included. --review by Harwood Simmons

in New York State School Music News, XXXV/5
(Jan. 1972) 24.

293. Gay, Albert I. Rhythmic Movement in Music Education
in the Elementary School, 1900 to 1940. Ed. D. dissertation, University of Michigan, 1966, 253 p. ;
LC 67-1744; DA XXVII/11A, 3891.
Determines the extent to which rhythmic movement
was included in the elementary school music program and
identifies various methods by which it was taught. Discusses
the influence of the physical education program, the kindergarten, and the eurhythmics of Jaques-Dalcroze.

294. Gehrkens, Karl W. "Rhythm Training and Dalcroze
Eurythmics." Yearbook of the Music Supervisors
National Conference, (1932) 306-10.
Discusses the techniques, value, philosophy, and
objectives of Dalcroze eurhythmics.

295. Gell, Heather. Music, Movement, and the Young Child.
Sydney: Australasian Publishing Co. , 1949, 196 p.

296. Glenn, Mabelle. "Demonstration of Creative Rhythm."
Yearbook of the Music Supervisors National Conference, (1932) 311-14.
Stresses that students should have much experience
with rhythm and bodily movement before the mathematical relationships of rhythm and meter are learned. Rhythmic
phrasing, pattern, and meter are discussed, and an outline
of a creative song project is given.

297. Grant, Ruth. "The Relation of Bodily Rhythm to Instrumental Music." Yearbook of the Music Educators National Conference, (1939-1940) 235-36.
A short description of bodily rhythmic activity in the
elementary grades.

298. Gray, Vera and Rachel Percival. Music, Movement
and Mime for Children. London: Oxford University
Press, 1962, 110 p.
A handbook for the classroom teacher which provides
follow-up work for use with the British Broadcasting Corpora-
tion's programs on music and movement. Appendixes include
suggestions for lessons based on time, weight, and space, and
a list of music suitable for accompanying movement.

299. Hall, Lucy D. "The Value of Eurythmics in Education."

Yearbook of the Music Educators National Conference, (1936) 150-53.
Explains the philosophy of the Jaques-Dalcroze system of eurhythmics and lists six objectives of rhythmic movement.   Describes eurhythmics as 1) a system of physical education which simultaneously develops the mind and satisfies
the aesthetic emotions, 2) a musical education which coordi-
nates bodily rhythms with those of music through rigorous
mental discipline, and 3) an intellectual training by way of
the arts and physical movement.

300.   Hughes, Dorothy T.   Rhythmic Games and Dances:
            Basic Activities for Elementary Grades.   New
            York: American Book Co. , 1942, 184 p.
            Includes children's dances, games and eurhythmics.
States that classroom rhythmic activity may be a significant
musical experience, "... or it may degenerate into mechanical meaningless motions.   Which it is depends largely upon
the teacher's own sense of appreciation and the ability to con-
vey this feeling to the pupils. "--p. 20.

301.   Humphreys, Louise and Jerrold Ross.   Interpreting
            Music through Movement.   Englewood Cliffs, NJ:
            Prentice-Hall, Inc. , 1964, 149 p.
            Contains verbal analyses of several works by six-
teen well-known composers.
                    Suggestions for responding to music creatively
                    through movement, on relating other subjects in
                    the arts, and for the development of listening. --
                    annotation in Collins (ed.), Music Education
                    Materials: ... , p. 97.

302.   Jaques-Dalcroze, Émile.   Eurhythmics, Art and Educa-
            tion.   Edited by Cynthia Cox.   Translated by
            Frederick Rothwell.   London: Chatto & Windus,
            1930, 265 p.
            A series of twenty-one articles written by Dalcroze
between 1922 and 1925.

303.   _____.   The Eurhythmics of Jaques-Dalcroze.   Bos-
            ton: Small, Maynard & Co. , 1918, 64 p.
            Contents include: "Note" by J. W. Harvey;   "In-
troduction" by M. E. Sadler;   "Rhythm as a Factor in Education, Moving Plastic and Dance" from lectures and addresses
by Emile Jaques-Dalcroze, translated by P. and E. Ingham;
"The Method: Growth and Practice" by P. B. Ingham;   "Lessons with Monsieur Dalcroze" by Ethel Ingham;   "The Value
of Eurhythmics to Art" by M. T. H. Sadler.

304. _____. Jaques-Dalcroze Method of Eurhythmics:
Rhythmic Movement. 2 vols. London: Novello &
Co., Ltd., Vol. I, 1920, 64 p.; Vol. II, 1921,
96 p.
 V 1: Development of the rhythmic & metric
 sense of the instinct for harmonious & balanced
 movements & of good motor habits. V 2: Bars
 of 6 to 9 beats & a chapter on the application of
 rhythmic movement to pianoforte technique. --
 annotation by Darrell in Schirmer's Guide to
 Books on Music and Musicians, p. 113.

305. _____. "Remarks or Arrhythmy." Translated by
Frederick Rothwell. Music and Letters, XIV/2
(Apr. 1933) 138-48.
 Defines arrhythmy (a term used by physicians to
describe the irregularity of cardiac contractions, but here
meaning "... any irregularity of the nervous and muscular
functions ... in time, in dynamics and in space."--p. 138),
notes its various manifestations in musicians, and suggests
the study of eurhythmics for its correction.

306. _____. Rhythm, Music and Education. Translated
by Harold F. Rubenstein. Rev. ed. Redcourt,
England: Dalcroze Society Inc., 1967, 200 p.
 A classic in the field of eurhythmics, first published
in 1921 but out of print since 1930. Consists of a collection
of articles, most of which appeared in Swiss and French periodicals from about 1900 to 1920. Contains the author's
principles and approach to eurhythmics as well as his ideas
on many other matters related to music education.
  Since the essays appear in chronological order,
  one can trace through them the development of
  Dalcroze's ideas through this period. The relationship of music and movement, which is the
  main theme of the book, is approached from
  many angles, both as a foundation for a general
  music training, and with reference to the more
  specific needs of dancers and other stage performers. --from review by Rupert Thackray in
  Music in Education, XXXI/327 (Sept. -Oct. 1967)
  580.

307. _____. "Rhythmics and Pianoforte Improvisation."
Translated by Frederick Rothwell. Music and Letters, XIII/4 (Oct. 1932) 371-80.
 Notes the advantages to be gained from the study of
improvisation and suggests that such instruction should be

based on eurhythmics.   An outline of improvisation activities
is given.

308.   Kitcat, Cecil; Hilda Schuster; and Susan T. Canfield.
        Curriculum for Dalcroze Eurhythmics in the Nursery
        School, Kindergarten and Grades I-VI.   The Com-
        mittee for the Revision of Music Curricula in the
        Elementary Schools of Pennsylvania, [n. d.], 8 p.
        (Mimeographed.)
        Contains a statement by Will Earhart on the value
and aims of the Dalcroze system of eurhythmics and outlines
suggestions for its use in public school music.

309.   Kuhn, Jacquelin C.   Thirty-Three Rhythms for Chil-
        dren: A Book of Text and Music for Children's
        Rhythmic Activities to be Used Primarily by Kin-
        dergarten and Primary Teachers and Parents.
        New York: Bregman, Vocco & Conn, 1956, 48 p.

310.   Maguire, Helena.   "On Eurhythmics. "   Musician,
        XIX/5 (May 1914) 309.
        A short history of the Dalcroze system and a de-
scription of its objectives and methods.

311.   Merlier, Elise de.   "Jaques-Dalcroze and Eurhythmics. "
        Musician, XIX/9 (Sept. 1914) 575-76.
        Discusses Dalcroze's system of eurhythmics and
gives descriptions and pictures of some of Dalcroze's eurhythmic group performances.

312.   Morgan, Bessie S.   "Musical Accompaniment: A Hand-
        book of Accompaniment for Teachers of Rhythmic
        Activities and Dance. "   Unpublished M. S. thesis,
        University of Wisconsin, 1947.
        The author's survey of accompaniment materials re-
sulted in this handbook of materials for piano and percussion
instruments.   Contains a score, musical examples, and helpful bibliography of related literature.

313.   Morgan, Esther and Hazel Grubbs.   "Approach to
        Rhythms for Children. "   Childhood Education,
        XXIX (Apr. 1953) 383-88.
        Describes a method of teaching rhythmic movement
to young children which, according to the authors, differs
from the traditional approach in that it does not set standards
of performance.   Emphasis is placed upon the individual
child; the teacher must be willing to serve as a guide rather
than a director.

Mursell, James L. Principles of Musical Education.
See No. 103.

314. Music Supervisors National Conference Research Coun-
        cil. Report. "Dalcroze Eurythmics." Yearbook
        of the Music Supervisors National Conference,
        (1930) 283-84.
        A concise explanation. Considers the inclusion of
eurhythmics in the school music curricula of the United States.

315. Pennington, Jo. The Importance of Being Rhythmic:
        A Study of the Principles of Dalcroze Eurythmics
        Applied to General Education and to the Arts of
        Music, Dancing and Acting. Based on and Adapted
        from "Rhythm, Music and Education," by Jaques-
        Dalcroze. New York: G. P. Putnam's Sons, 1925,
        142 p.
        Includes definitions of eurhythmics and surveys the
origin and history of the Dalcroze method. Chapter VII,
"Rhythmic Training for the Musician," discusses the aims and
values of eurhythmics in music education. A list of private
and special schools in the United States which teach Dalcroze
eurhythmics is appended.

316. Revelli, William D. "What about Rhythm?" Etude,
        LXXIII/5 (May 1955) 19, 56.
        Defines rhythm, meter, tempo, time, and beat.
Urges music educators to give students training in bodily and
physical response to rhythmic patterns.

317. Rosenstrauch, Henrietta. "Rhythmic Problems in
        Music Teaching." Proceedings of the Music
        Teachers National Association, (1946) 342-49.
        Recommends rhythmic training which employs mus-
cular experience, particularly the Dalcroze method of eurhythmics. Calls for more cooperation between Dalcroze teachers
and instrumental teachers.

318. Saffran, Rosanna B. First Book of Creative Rhythms.
        New York: Holt, Rinehart and Winston, Inc., 1963,
        152 p.
        Presents a systematic method for developing natural
body responses in primary grade children. Following three
introductory chapters, each of the remaining chapters is devoted to a basic rhythmic movement. Includes numerous
examples of piano accompaniments to rhythmic movement.

319. Sarvis, Portia. <u>An Analytical Study of Accompaniment</u>
       <u>for Rhythms</u>. Ed. D. dissertation, University of
       California, 1966, 163 p. ; LC 67-4497; DA XXVII/
       10A, 3237.
            Develops a classroom teacher's guide for accom-
panying rhythms creatively in the elementary school. Contains a review of related literature and analyzes the function
of accompaniment, the relationships between movement and
music, and the techniques of effectively accompanying specific
kinds of movement by means of the piano, percussion instruments, songs, and verbal accompaniment.

320. Schreiber, Avis T. "Rhythmic Development in the
       Public Schools." <u>Yearbook of the Music Educators</u>
       <u>National Conference</u>, (1936) 153-54.
            Stresses that children should be allowed to freely
express their ideas through rhythmic movement according to
the nature of the music they hear, without first being told
what to do by adults.

321. Schultz, E. J. "Fundamental Experiences in Rhythm."
       <u>Educational Music Magazine</u>, XXXII (Jan. -Feb. 1953)
       16-17.
            States that rhythm should be experienced by the pu-
pil through physical activity before rhythmic notation is taught.
Seven physical activities are suggested.

322. Schuster, Hilda M. "The Aesthetic Contributions of
       Dalcroze Eurhythmics to Modern American Educa-
       tion." Unpublished M. S. thesis, Duquesne Univer-
       sity, 1938, 65 p.
            Sketches the biography of Émile Jaques-Dalcroze
and discusses the meaning, objectives, importance, development, and contributions of his system of eurhythmics in
Europe and the United States.

323. Shafer, Mary S. and Mary M. Mosher. <u>Rhythms for</u>
       <u>Children</u>. New York: Ronald Press Co. , 1921,
       48 p.
            Outlines physiological and psychological character-
istics and developmental goals and values for children in the
first and second grades. Forty-four short, original piano
accompaniments to suggested rhythmic activities are included,
with such titles as "Skip No. 1," "Quiet Walk," and "Running
and Jumping. "

       Swindle, P. F. "On the Inheritance of Rhythm. " See
No. 161.

324. Tellier, Barbara S. "Rhythm is a Feeling." Instru-
        mentalist, XX/11 (June 1966) 28-34.
      Maintains that strong rhythmic motions or energetic
counting aloud will instill in a student a rhythmic feeling that
can later be muted to an inward, steady rhythmic sense.
Suggests some novel solutions to common rhythmic problems.

325. Waterman, Elizabeth. The A B C of Rhythmic Train-
        ing: A Course in the Correlation of Music and
        Movement. Chicago: Clayton F. Summy Co.,
        1927, 148 p.
      Contains graded procedures and music for rhythmic
movement for the first four grades.

326. _____. The Rhythm Book. New York: A. S.
        Barnes & Co., Inc., 1937.

327. Whitlock, Virginia. Come and Caper: Creative
        Rhythms, Pantomimes, and Plays, with Music by
        Various Composers. New York: G. Schirmer,
        Inc., 1932, 134 p.
        Music with extensive notes and illustrations on
        the rhythmic and interpretative activities de-
        veloped for 1st-to-8th grade children at the
        Lincoln School of Teachers College, Columbia
        University, New York. --annotation by Darrell
        in Schirmer's Guide to Books on Music and
        Musicians, p. 92.

328. Williams, Marian S. "Rhythm in the Elementary
        Music Program." Unpublished M.M. thesis,
        Northwestern University, 1938, 37 p.
      Decries the neglect of rhythmic training and recom-
mends the Dalcroze approach. Suggests classroom activities,
general teaching procedures, and materials.

329. Williamson, John F. "Rhythm Makes the Music Go."
        Etude, LXIX/1 (Jan. 1951) 18, 61.
      Discusses teaching rhythms to choirs by having the
singers clap the rhythms before singing them.

330. Wilson, Grace V. "A Rhythmic Program in Elemen-
        tary Schools." Yearbook of the Music Educators
        National Conference, (1937) 158-60.
      Espouses bodily movement for teaching rhythm and
acknowledges her own mistake in trying to teach rhythm
arithmetically.

C. Rhythm Band

        Participation in the rhythm band (also called per-
cussion band or rhythm orchestra) is an approach often used
with young children as soon as they are able to react to pulse
and tempo. This activity develops fundamental rhythmic
skills, stimulates interest in instrumental music, and provides a means of self-expression and creativity. (The recent introduction of Orff and Kodály techniques has taken
some emphasis away from the traditional rhythm band approach.)
        For experimental research which comments on the
educational value of rhythm band instruments, see Tietze's
Ph. D. dissertation (No. 357). One of the best up-to-date,
comprehensive discussions is contained in Marguerite V.
Hood's Teaching Rhythm and Using Classroom Instruments
(No. 217), Part II, especially Chapter V.

331.   Adair, Y.   Music through the Percussion Band.   New
            York: Boosey & Hawkes, Inc. , 1952, 225 p.
        Intended for use with children seven to ten or more
years of age.   French time-names are used throughout.   The
pulse is limited to the quarter or dotted quarter note.   Contains advice on the care and technique of the instruments and
an appendix giving a graded list of music.
            Review by E. A. Faunt in Canadian Music Journal,
I/ 2 (Winter 1957) 73-75.

332.   _____. "Musical Examples for Percussion Band
            Exercises."   Music Teacher, XXXIV (May 1955)
            249.

333.   Clemens, James R.   An Invitation to Rhythm.
            Dubuque, IA: W. C. Brown Co, 1962, 164 p.
        A creative approach to constructing and using
rhythm instruments for children from pre-school to age
eleven.   Relates movement to sound.   Contains useful suggestions, illustrations, examples, bibliographies and dis-
cographies.

334.   Diller, Angela and Kate S. Page. How to Teach the
          Rhythm-Band. New York: G. Schirmer, Inc.,
          1928, 23 p.
     Describes how the rhythm band can serve as prep-
aration for the school orchestra or band.

335.   Echols, L. W.   "Rhythm Bands for Elementary School
          Teachers." School Musician, XXIV (Nov. 1952)
          8-9.

336.   Everett, Edna. Rhythm Band Music for Small Players.
          Chicago: Beckley-Cardy Co., 1941, 47 p.
          Briefly discusses the rhythm band and its instru-
ments. Contains descriptive music and suggested recitations
for rhythm band programs.

337.   Fitzsimmons, Grace. "A Rhythm Orchestra." Edu-
          cational Music Magazine, XXXII (Sept.-Oct. 1952)
          25.
          Gives some procedures used by the author in di-
recting a rhythm band.

338.   Handbook for Beginning and Advanced Rhythm Bands.
          Elkhart, IN: C. G. Conn, Ltd., Pan-American
          Band Instrument Division, 1951, 49 p.
          Organization, rehearsal room, seating plan, cor-
          rect playing positions, scoring, and class pro-
          cedure for grades one, two, and three are
          covered.... Playing positions are clearly illus-
          trated by photographs. There are some 50 or
          more musical selections given, showing notation
          for melody and percussion.--review in Instru-
          mentalist, VI/1 (Sept. 1951) 31.

339.   Hannen, Helen M. "The Relationship between the
          Rhythm Band and the Study of Instruments in the
          Band and Orchestra." Yearbook of the Music
          Educators National Conference, (1939-1940) 232-33.
          Reports the results of an MENC committee survey
on the rhythm band as part of the school instrumental program, and as part of music appreciation. Musical, social,
and physical values gained from this activity are listed.

340.   Hawkinson, John and Martha Faulhaber. Rhythms,
          Music and Instruments to Make. Chicago: Whit-
          man, Albert & Co., 1970.

341. Krawitz, Ida S. How to Teach Rhythms and Rhythm
      Bands: Fifteen Lessons in Fundamental Rhythm
      Training. New York: G. Schirmer, Inc., 1955,
      69 p.
      ... designed to guide the teacher of young chil-
      dren through the beginning lessons of rhythms
      and rhythm bands. The lessons are planned for
      one period each week and are based on material
      worked out with the children of the Settlement
      Music School, Philadelphia, Pennsylvania. --from
      Foreword.
      Contains piano music and teaching procedures.

342. Lemke, G. "Teaching Rhythm Bands in Rural Schools."
      School Musician, XXVI (Jan. 1955) 14-15.

343. Mirchin, Eva. Let's Have a Rhythm Band. Fort
      Worth, TX: Rhythm Band, Inc.

344. _____. Let's Lead a Rhythm Band. Fort Worth,
      TX: Rhythm Band, Inc.

345. Music Supervisors National Conference Research Coun-
      cil. Report. "The Rhythm Orchestra." Yearbook
      of the Music Supervisors National Conference,
      (1930) 284-85.
      Describes the state of the rhythm orchestra in the
schools and discusses its educational values.
      Dates the idea of the rhythm orchestra back to the
Kindersinfonie often ascribed to (Franz) Joseph Haydn. Since
this article was published, musicological research has un-
covered evidence which attributes this work both to Leopold
Mozart and Johann Michael Haydn. See H. C. Robbins Landon, The Symphonies of Joseph Haydn (London: Universal Edition Ltd., 1953), pp. 803-4; H. C. Robbins Landon, Supplement to the Symphonies of Joseph Haydn (London: Barrie and
Rockliff, 1961), pp. 27-28; and Karl Geiringer and Irene
Geiringer, Haydn: A Creative Life in Music, Rev. ed.
(Berkeley: University of California Press, 1968 [c1963]),
p. 316.
      Also called Toy Symphony and Berdoltsgadner
Sinfonia, this composition is scored for first and second
violins, double bass, and "toy" instruments such as cuckoo,
quail, nightingale, drum, rattle, and triangle.

346. Novich, Clara K. "Start the Children with Rhythm."
      Etude, LX/9 (Sept. 1942) 596, 634.

Offers general comments on organizing and training a rhythm band. A selected list of pieces using different combinations of rhythm instruments is included.

347. Pearman, Martha. "Percussion in the Classroom."
     Percussionist, V/2 (Dec. 1967) 262-66.
     Suggests using percussion instruments to teach concepts such as tempo, accent, dynamics, syncopation, and rhythmic subdivision; to develop improvisational skills and creativity; and to encourage personal involvement of each child. Objects to the use of plastic or cheap imitations of percussion instruments often used in rhythm bands.

348. Pew, Florine. "We Clapped Our Hands." Music
     Educators Journal, LI/6 (June-July 1965) 72, 75.
     A description of rhythm band procedures.

349. Roeslein, Adelaide K. "Toy Symphony." Etude,
     LXX/8 (Aug. 1952) 14, 56.
     Gives suggestions on selection and construction of rhythm instruments.

350. Rusette, Louie E. de. Children's Percussion Bands.
     2nd ed. London: K. Paul, Trench, Trubner & Co.,
     Ltd., 1930, 173 p.
     Divides percussion band activities into three stages: 1) pulse perception and rhythmic freedom, 2) pitch perception and mood response, and 3) harmonic perception and introduction of notation. Lists of band equipment and music for the percussion band are given.

351. St. Quentin, Irene. Toy-Symphony Orchestras and How
     They May Be Developed. Boston: O. Ditson Co.,
     1928, 30 p.

352. Schultz, Ernest J. "Are You Tapping the Rich Resources in Rhythm Bands?" Instrumentalist, VII/5
     (Mar.-Apr. 1953) 52-54.
     Outlines several phases of rhythm band procedures from rote imitation to combining orchestral and band instruments with the rhythm band.

353. Squire, Russel N. "Enjoying Music through Rhythm."
     Educational Music Magazine, XXVIII (Jan.-Feb.
     1949) 14-15.
     Suggests teaching a basic feeling for rhythm to children eight to ten years old through participation in rhythm bands.

354. Standard Rhythm Band Instruction Book. Fort Worth,
      TX: Rhythm Band, Inc.

355. Stickle, Mary L. The Toy Symphony: A Teacher's
      Manual. Boston: C. C. Birchard & Co. , 1930,
      24 p.
      "Instructions for playing by the rote method; ac-
companying an instrumental book ... of song & toy-symphony
orchestrations. "--annotation by Darrell in Schirmer's Guide
to Books on Music and Musicians, p. 60.

356. Synnberg, Margaret J. New Rhythm Band Method.
      Chicago: M. M. Cole Publishing Co. , 1937, 16 p.
      Offers a brief description of the nature of the
rhythm band, discusses its instrumentation, organization,
accompaniment, repertory, and conducting technique, and contains rhythm band scores to nine familiar folk and nursery
songs.

357. Tietze, William B. The Effect of Pre-Band Melody
      and Rhythm Instruments on the Musical Learning of
      Beginning Fourth Grade Instrumental Students.
      Ph. D. dissertation, State University of Iowa, 1958,
      102 p. ; LC 58-5868; DA XIX/8, 2103.
      An experimental study which concludes that there is
significant value in teaching beginning instrumental music students the individual components of music, rhythm, and note
and rest values before starting them on band instruments;
there is carry-over of musical knowledge acquired in pre-
band instrument classes; and there is improvement in atti-
tudes and interests of those students who participate in such
a program.

358. Vandevere, J. Lilian. "The Rhythm Orchestra's
      Place. " Yearbook of the Music Supervisors Na-
      tional Conference, (1933) 150-52.
      Discusses the purpose, values, and creative aspects
of the rhythm orchestra. Suggests instruments to use. Correlates rhythm activities with other school subjects.

359. _____. The Toy Symphony Orchestra: Its Organi-
      zation and Training. Boston: C. C. Birchard &
      Co. , 1927, 22 p.
      A brief treatment. Contains a list of graded music,
instructions for making instruments and suggested teaching
procedures.

360. Vernazza, Marcelle. Making and Playing Classroom
     Instruments. San Francisco: Fearon Publishers,
     1959, 28 p.

361. Votaw, Lyravine. Rhythm Band Direction. Chicago:
     Ludwig & Ludwig, [n. d.], 43 p.

362. Williams, John M. and Helen E. Brady. A First Book
     for Rhythm Band. Boston: Boston Music Co.,
     1930, 17 p.
     Music arranged from the pieces in John M. Williams'
class piano method.

363. Zanzig, Augustus D. Starting and Developing a Rhythm
     Band. New York: National Recreation Association,
     1937, 24 p.
     Straightforward advice, with lists of recommended
     scores & recordings, and information on making
     & buying instruments. --annotation by Darrell in
     Schirmer's Guide to Books on Music and Musi-
     cians, p. 60.

D. Miscellaneous Approaches

     Collected here are writings which discuss often
interrelated approaches to teaching rhythm. Aids such as
the following are included: mathematical concepts, numbers,
arrows, pulse subdivisions, foot tap, syllables, words, songs,
time-names, and mnemonic devices. Periodical articles pre-
dominate the literature in this section. Attention should be
called to the early discussion of French time-names by Chevé
(No. 371).

364. Axton, Charles B. II. The Use of Previously Learned
     Mathematics Concepts to Introduce Concepts of
     Rhythm Notation to Third-Grade Children. Ph. D.
     dissertation, University of Kansas, 1969, 129 p.;
     LC 69-21,488; DA XXX/7A, 3036.
     Finds that
         ... concepts of rhythm notation are more easily
         acquired when they are related to previously

learned mathematics concepts than when such as-
sociations are not made. --from DA XXX/7A,
3036.

365.   Baker, J. Percy. "Why Is There So Much Bad Time?"
       Etude, XLIII/1 (Jan. 1925) 19-20.
       Suggests a procedure for teaching simple rhythms
using the Galin-Paris-Chevé time-names.

366.   Barnett, David. "Harmonic Rhythm and Mother Goose."
       Music Educators Journal, XLV, (June-July 1959)
       20-22.
       Illustrates the
       ... resemblance between the patterns of har-
       monic rhythm appearing in art-compositions and
       the rhythmic patterns on which the nonsense-
       lines of Mother Goose or of folk-song are based.
       --p. 20.

367.   Bay, Adela. "The Time Problem." Music Educators
       Journal, LIII/2 (Oct. 1966) 73-77.
       Suggests a clock-oriented method of teaching rhythm.
The note heads of the rhythm are distributed proportionately
along the circumference of the clock; the note stems are di-
rected towards the clock's center. The author asserts that
this method will solve the problems of counting dotted notes
and syncopation.

368.   Beck, William. "Are the Arrows Misleading the
       Students?" Instrumentalist, XXII/8 (Mar. 1968)
       33-34.
       Notes some confusing aspects of using arrows to
teach rhythm and states that the arrow is not representative
of where the beat actually begins or ends. Discusses dotted
rhythms.

369.   Benham, John L. Rhythm Pedagogy by Syllabic Imita-
       tion through Conceptualization of Regular and Ir-
       regular Metric and Beat Subdivisions. Ed. D. dis-
       sertation, University of Northern Colorado, 1971,
       101 p.; LC 71-26,807; DA XXXII/5A, 2724-25.
       Formulates a pedagogy of rhythm instruction based
upon conceptual understanding and a consistent approach to
rhythm performance by syllabic imitation. Gives four basic
syllable combinations which may be adapted to fit nearly all
rhythmic patterns in regular and irregular metric and beat
subdivisions. The rest, tie, and dot are given the same

amount of pedagogical consideration as note values in the syllabization of counting and are used as the basis for teaching
the concepts of extrametrical and irregular beat subdivision.

370. Cantwell, Donald C. "The Use of Mnemonics in Music
     Reading." Music Educators Journal, XXXVIII
     (Nov.-Dec. 1951) 52.
         Asserts that "Music reading can be made easier for
the beginning student through the use of mnemonics, ..."
For triplet rhythms, the author suggests using the words
"Hop-a-long Cass-i-dy"; for four sixteenth notes, the word
"Mis-sis-sip-pi."

371. Chevé, Emile J. M. The Theory of Music. Trans-
     lated and appendixes added by George W. Bullen.
     2nd ed. London: Moffatt & Paige, 18??, 174 p.
         This is the first English translation of the second
French edition, which appeared in 1844. The work is based
upon the pedagogical approach of Pierre Galin and Aimé
Paris. It is included because of its extensive influence on
more recent methods of counting rhythm. Part II, "Time,"
offers an unusually complete explanation of French time-
names. Pages 69-70 contain a table compiled by Galin called
the Chronomerist which shows divisions and subdivisions of
the beat, together with the time-names proposed by Paris
which are placed under each of the notes. For the conve-
nience of the reader, the table is included as Appendix of
this bibliography.

372. Cobb, Hazel. "Rhythm--Easy as Pie." Clavier, I/1
     (1962) 18.
         Offers visual and mnemonic aids for teaching
rhythms utilizing the basic word "pie." Words such as
apple, gooseberry, chocolate, and huckleberry represent subdivisions of the beat. This is a more unified system than
most because one word expresses a "whole count" whether
the "count" has one or more notes.

373. D'Angelo, Donald. "Teaching Rhythm--A Symposium:
     II. A New Twist to Teaching Rhythm." Instru-
     mentalist, XXIII/2 (Sept. 1968) 64-65.
         Suggests teaching rhythm by graphically representing
the subdivisions of the beat by arrows and rhythmic syllables.
The title is misleading; the approach is traditional.

374. Dixon, Dean. "Solving Rhythmic Problems." Music
     Educators Journal, XXX/6 (May-June 1944) 36-38.

Presents the author's system of counting which he
claims will immediately and infallibly produce mathematically
correct rhythmic responses. The system uses three steps:
"(1) Disregarding the given time signature. (2) Using the
fastest frequently recurring note as a sort of lowest-common-
denominator and making it the unit of counting. (3) COUNTING
BACKWARDS."--p. 36.

Example 7 in the article illustrates this system:

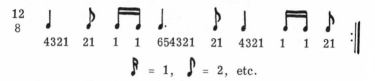

The author states that the system has worked successfully in almost every musical situation, but offers no
statistical proof of this.

375. Drake, Alan H.   An Experimental Study of Selected
        Variables in the Performance of Musical Durational
        Notation.   Ph.D. dissertation, Florida State Univer-
        sity, 1965, 110 p.; LC 65-15,456; DA XXVI/8,
        4712-13.

Measures and compares the variables of beat reproduction, beat steadiness, and beat subdivision accuracy in performances of musical durational notation by thirty-two college
freshman band members. The performances were tapped on
a key, recorded on tape, transferred to visual form, and
analyzed. The study assesses the influence upon these variables of inducing the subjects to use imaged subdivisions of
the beat and finds that such inducement may cause an overall
numerical improvement in beat steadiness and beat subdivision
accuracy, but the amount of the improvement attributable to
this treatment is not statistically significant.

376. _____.   "An Experimental Study of Selected Variables
        in the Performance of Musical Durational Notation."
        Journal of Research in Music Education, XVI/4
        (Winter 1968) 329-38.

Based on the author's doctoral dissertation (see
No. 375).

377. Fletcher, Stanley.   "Rhythm and Metrical Bookkeeping."
        Clavier, II/2 (Mar.-Apr. 1963) 18-21.

States that counting is a way of keeping track of
rhythmic consciousness by analyzing it metrically.

Recommends a counting method which could be extremely confusing to beginning students.

378.   Gillespie, George D.   "The Set Theory for Music."
           Instrumentalist, XX/5 (Dec. 1965) 6, 10.
           Suggests utilizing simple mathematical set theory to
explain basic rhythmic relationships.

       Gordon, Edwin.   The Psychology of Music Teaching.
See No. 98.

379.   Hoover, Walter.   "Foot Patting Helpful for Rhythm
           Problems."   Instrumentalist, VIII/4 (Dec. 1953) 4.
           Describes the "single foot tap" and the "two-foot
tap" for beginning students.

380.   _____.   "Teaching Rhythm--A Symposium: I.   An
           Approach to Rhythm."   Instrumentalist, XXIII/2
           (Sept. 1968) 59-62.
           Presents the author's approach to teaching rhythm
by the foot tap method and lists some of its advantages.   The
discussion is marred by several instances of unclear diagrams
and explanations.

381.   Jenkins, Harry.   "Teaching Syncopation."   Instrumen-
           talist, XXI/7 (Feb. 1967) 57.
           Suggests and illustrates the notation of syncopated
rhythm so the normal pulse is apparent.

382.   Kohut, Daniel.   "Any Rhythm Problems?"   Instrumen-
           talist, XIX/7 (Feb. 1965) 68-71.
           Offers a pedagogical approach to rhythm using the
foot-tap, arrows, and words.

383.   Lacy, Gene.   "Contemporary Music--Solving the Prob-
           lems in High School Groups."   Instrumentalist,
           XXIV/8 (Mar. 1970) 36-37.
           Suggests using scales for drilling multimeters and
multirhythms.

384.   Laycock, Ralph G.   "Competent, Conscientious, Con-
           stant Counting."   Instrumentalist, XX/5 (Dec.
           1965) 73-77.
           Discusses musical benefits to be derived from
counting and offers a nine-step plan for achieving rhythmic
understanding and security.

385.   Lesueur, Alexander.   "Articulation-Rhythm Problems."
            Instrumentalist, XXIV/4 (Nov. 1969) 82.
        Discusses articulation patterns which are the fre-
quent cause of rhythmic problems for wind instrumentalists.
Lengthening the first note of a slur and "leading one beat
into the next" are offered as solutions to the problems.

386.   Maxson, Frederick.   "The Use of Words and Syllables
            in the Study of Rhythm." Musician, XVIII/1 (Jan.
            1913) 17.
        A short discussion; various words are suggested
for use in teaching up to six subdivisions of the beat and for
the "two against three" rhythm.

387.   Miessner, W. Otto.   "How to Master Rhythms."
            Music Educators Journal, LIII/3 (Nov. 1966) 48-49.
        Traces the history of the Rhythophone, an invention
of the author.   Suggests learning a difficult rhythm by listening to it repeatedly, expressing it using the syllable "ta,"
drumming it with the hand, singing it, and finally playing it.

388.   _____.   "How to Think Rhythms." Music Educators
            Journal, XLIX/6 (June-July) 37-40.
        Discusses the evolution and development of a system
of mnemonics to aid in perceiving, feeling, and expressing
rhythms.

389.   Ott, Joseph.   "Studies in Polyrhythms." Instrumen-
            talist, XXI/8 (Mar. 1967) 65.
        Discusses the performance of polyrhythms and pre-
sents a plan for teaching them based on double and triple
beat subdivisions.

390.   Palmer, Edith M.   "The Effect of Various Backgrounds
            upon Rhythmic Patterns." Unpublished M. M. thesis,
            Eastman School of Music, University of Rochester,
            1933, 35 p.
        A study which demonstrates the validity of the
method of teaching rhythm which was used at the Eastman
School of Music.   The method utilizes regular divisions and
subdivisions ("background") of the pulse.   A test was constructed which determined the effect of various backgrounds
upon the rhythmic performance of seventy-five members of
freshman theory classes at Eastman.   Subjects tapped rhythms
using a metal plate and stylus.

391.   Pickens, Blanchard.   "The Teaching of Rhythm to

Instrumental Music Students. " Unpublished M. A.
thesis, Ohio State University, 1941, 67 p.
   Presents several psychologists' theories on the perception of rhythm and a scheme for the analysis of musical
rhythm. Proposes a plan of rhythmic training through the
song approach for melody instrument classes.

392. Pizer, Russell. "Teaching Rhythm--A Symposium:
      V. Toward More Accurate Rhythm. " Instrumen-
      talist, XXIII/2 (Sept. 1968) 75-76.
   Discusses possible problems arising from an incorrect use of the foot tap and various words to indicate the
subdivisions of the beat.

393. Porter, Alma L. "An Evaluation of Two Approaches
      to Teaching Rhythm. " Unpublished M. A. thesis,
      Ohio State University, 1946, 73 p.
   Fifth and sixth grade students were instructed in a
notation reading approach and a song approach and then tested
for ability to clap the rhythm of a song. The song approach
was claimed superior, but no level of significance of the
study was indicated.

394. Rainbow, Bernarr. "Why French Time-Names?"
      Music in Education, XXVII/303 (Sept. 1963) 137-38.
   Briefly traces the development of French time-names
from their origin in the French military band to their English
adaptation by John Curwen. Proposes a set of time-names
which could be learned more readily by English-speaking students.

395. Reichenthal, Eugene. "French Time Names. " Music
      Education in Action. Edited by Archie N. Jones.
      Boston: Allyn & Bacon, Inc. , 1960, pp. 319-24.
   A brief history and explanation of French time-
names. Surveys "... the four most popular methods for
teaching rhythm in the United States ... ": the simple definition, action words, mnemonic words, and number-counting
systems. Includes suggestions and techniques for teaching
French time-names.

396. Revelli, William D. "To Beat or Not To Beat?"
      Etude, LXXIII/6 (June 1955) 19, 48.
   Emphasizes the need for rhythmic training in the
public school instrumental music program. Describes the
advantages and disadvantages of three approaches to developing
rhythm in students: thinking the rhythm without any physical

response, counting by tapping the foot, and counting out loud.
It is suggested that tapping the foot has the most advantages.

397.   Roberts, Alfred L.   "Analyses of Vocabulary and
          Rhythm Patterns in Songs from Selected Elementary
          School Music Books." Unpublished Ed. D. disserta-
          tion, University of Wyoming, 1963, 139 p.
       Music books from four basic music series used in
grades one through four were examined to determine whether
or not the rhythmic patterns in the texts were presented frequently enough to encourage retention and the development of
music reading skills.   The suitability of the language vocabulary for each grade level and the possibilities of using the
texts for remedial reading activities are discussed.

398.   Scholtz, Francis N.   "Teaching Rhythm."   Musart,
          XIX/4 (Feb.-Mar. 1967) 42-45.
       Suggests a mathematical approach to counting and
the use of the foot-tap.

399.   Sorlien, Leon C.   " 'Rithmetic and Rhythm--Are Closely
          Related and Can Be Used together in Systematic
          Drill." Instrumentalist, VI/2 (Oct. 1951) 10-11.
       Offers a counting system which uses the foot-tap,
compares rhythmic subdivisions to dollars and cents values,
and suggests using the word "merrily" for triplets.

400.   Stetson, R. B.   "The Teaching of Rhythm." Musical
          Quarterly, IX/2 (Apr. 1923) 181-90.
       Suggests teaching simple rhythms by making use of
familiar poetry and Mother Goose rhymes.

401.   Stone, Marion B.   "Reading Rhythm." Clavier, X/8
          (Nov. 1971) 6-12.
       A valuable collection of ideas on teaching rhythm.
Discusses the use of deductive reasoning and spatial and visual aids, such as outlining the rhythm of the measure, vertical alignment of notes when reading two staves at once, and
figuring out the rhythm in difficult measures by reading it
backwards.   The points made are illustrated by twenty-six
musical examples from the piano literature.

402.   Stoutamire, Albert L.   "Teaching Rhythmic Notation."
          Music Educators Journal, LI/2 (Nov.-Dec. 1964)
          91-95.
       Presents the author's method of teaching basic sub-
divisions of "duple" and "triple" "time-unit" meters.

Recommends a variation of a common counting system in a manner which is confusing because of incomplete explanations and typographical errors.

403. Tenaglia, Richard. "Teaching Counting with the New
      Math." Instrumentalist, XXII/3 (Oct. 1967) 47-50.
      Offers suggestions and gives a chart for teaching
rhythmic counting by relating rhythms to arithmetical equiva-
lencies and terminology used in teaching "new math." Briefly
discusses the terminology of Traugott Rohner's Mūsica (see
also No. 68).

404. Triplett, Norman and Edmund C. Sanford. "Studies of
      Rhythm and Meter." American Journal of Psy-
      chology, XII (Apr. 1901) 361-87.
      Examines stanza forms and rhythms of nursery
rhymes and college yells. Includes a brief collection of common rhythms with words that have been fitted to them.

405. Weidner, Robert W. "Outflanking the 8th Note."
      Instrumentalist, XV/4 (Dec. 1960) 36-37.
      Presents some syllables to use in teaching eighth
notes and triplet-eighth notes.

E. Innovative Approaches

        The approaches described in this section have

evolved largely as a result of the application of technological

"hardware" to the problems of teaching rhythm. The litera-

ture deals with programed learning, teaching machines,

tachistoscopic techniques, and devices for measuring rhythmic

performance such as the Iowa Piano Camera (see No. 408)

and the rhythm-meter (see No. 412).

406. Christ, William B. The Reading of Rhythm Notation
      Approached Experimentally According to Techniques
      and Principles of Word Reading. Ph.D. disserta-
      tion, Indiana University, 1954, 108 p. ; LC A54-
      986; DA XIV/4, 684.
      Finds that rhythmic reading drill with the tachisto-
scope and metronome is a quick, efficient means of developing the ability to perceive and reproduce rhythm patterns.

Review by John W. Shepard in Council for Research
in Music Education Bulletin, No. 7 (Spring 1966) 78-82.

407.   Dallin, Leon.   Introduction to Music Reading: A Pro-
       gram for Personal Instruction.   Glenview, IL:
       Scott, Foresman & Co., 1966, 146 p.
       A programed text designed for those who have had
no previous musical instruction.   Its behavioral objectives as
stated in the Preface are "... to read music notation, to
pick out simple melodies on the piano, to follow printed music as it is played, and to use the basic terminology in talk-
ing and writing about music."   The book is divided into two
units of study: rhythm and pitch.   Fifty-one pages are devoted to rhythm.   Covers note and rest durations from double
whole to sixty-fourth, simple (binary) and compound (ternary)
meter signatures, divisions from duplet to septuplet, and
syncopation.   Employs the foot-tap in order to leave the voice
free to sing and the hands free to clap other rhythms or play
an instrument.   Includes a brief supplementary section which
explains terms and symbols not contained in the main body of
the book.   The language used and the self-evaluation required
would seem to restrict its use to students of high school age
and older.
       Review by Sara Holroyd in Journal of Research in
Music Education, XV/2 (Summer 1967) 168-69;   Charles L.
Spohn in Music Educators Journal, LIII/2 (Oct. 1966) 92-95.

408.   Henderson, M. T.   "Rhythmic Organization in Artistic
       Piano Performance."   Objective Analysis of Musical
       Performance.   Studies in the Psychology of Music,
       Vol. IV.   Edited by Carl E. Seashore.   Iowa City,
       IA: University Press, 1936, pp. 281-305.
       Performances of Chopin's Nocturne in G Minor,
Op. 15, No. 3 by two music faculty members at Iowa University were recorded and graphed by the Iowa Piano Camera.
Factors analyzed which are related to the present study include rhythm, accentuation, duration, sentence and phrase
rubato, chord synchronization, synchronization of melody and
accompaniment, and the relation of duration to pedaling.

409.   Ihrke, Walter R.   An Experimental Study of the Ef-
       fectiveness and Validity of an Automated Rhythm
       Training Program.   Final Report.   U.S. Office of
       Education Cooperative Research Project 8-A-008,
       University of Connecticut, 1969, 150 p.;   ED 032
       790.
       A study was devised to determine the validity

and effectiveness of applying automation comcpets
[sic] to rhythm instruction in music. Students
from two semesters of a music class for the
classroom teacher were divided randomly into
experimental and control groups. ... The experimental group read music from a training manual,
listened to a two-channel tape consisting of background music and model rhythm music, played a
rhythmic sequence to the background music on
an organ, and received feedback indicating rhythmic errors from an electronic rhythm monitor.
Control group students received traditional
course instruction. ... Man-Whitney U-test results showed a high degree of effectiveness and
validity, indicating that automated rhythm training techniques are a useful supplement to music
instruction. A rhythm training manual which was
developed for the project is included. --from abstract in Research in Education, V/2 (Feb. 1970)
52-53.

See also the following articles by the author: "Auto-
mated Music Training," Journal of Research in Music Educa-
tion, X/1 (Spring 1963) 3-20; "Automated Music Training,"
Council for Research in Music Education Bulletin, No. 2
(Winter 1964) 6-8; "Automated Music Training: Final Re-
port on Phase One," Journal of Research in Music Education,
XIX/4 (Winter 1971) 474-80; "Automated Rhythm Training:
Progress Report," Council for Research in Music Education
Bulletin, No. 7 (Spring 1966) 34-37; "Programed Rhythm
Training in Automated Music Training," Journal of the Na-
tional Society for Programed Instruction, VII (Sept. 1968).

410. McArthur, William F. , Jr. A Program of Instruction
        in Fundamental Rhythm, Using the Language Master,
        an Audiovisual Instructional Device. Ph.D. disser-
        tation, University of Alabama, 1969, 128 p. ;
        LC 70-9368; DA XXX/12A, 5473.
An experimental study concerned with beginning music students at the junior high level. Findings indicate that
fundamental rhythmic concepts and skills as an extracted
separate entity are better learned by using a logically-se-
quenced program presented by a machine than by using conventional methods and a teacher.

        Magnell, Elmer. "Teaching Rhythm--A Symposium:
III. Systems for Reading Rhythm at Sight. " See No. 230.

411.   Mears, Wilfred G.   <u>Tri-Sensory Reinforcement of a</u>
        <u>Rhythm Learning Program.</u>   Ed. D. dissertation,
        Flordia State University, 1965, 136 p. ;   LC 65-
        15,477;   DA XXVI/ 8, 4717-18.
        An IBM card punch console was programed to pre-
sent rhythmic stimulation and reinforcement in verbal, notational, aural, and tactile modes, and in combinations of these
modes to the degree that subjects employing machine functions
were able to show change in rhythmic understanding.

412.   Seashore, Carl E.   <u>The Present Status of Research in</u>
        <u>the Psychology of Music at the University of Iowa.</u>
        University of Iowa Studies, Series on Aims and
        Progress of Research, Vol. II, No. 4, Iowa City,
        IA: University of Iowa, June 15, 1928.
        The "rhythm-meter" is described as
            ... an electric apparatus which records graph-
            ically the exact performance in any rhythmic
            pattern.   The norm for performance is indicated
            on the instrument and the degree of error in
            each note that is played appears in the graphic
            record of the entire performance. --p. 17.
Thus, the machine shows the musician the nature of his error
and serves as a standard for emulation.

413.   Shrader, David L.   <u>An Aural Approach to Rhythmic</u>
        <u>Sight Reading Based Upon Principles of Programed</u>
        <u>Learning, Utilizing a Stereo-Tape Teaching Machine.</u>
        D. M. A. dissertation, University of Oregon, 1970,
        161 p. ;   LC 70-21,576;   DA XXXI/ 5A, 2426.
        Designs, constructs, and tests a programed method
of rhythmic instruction on the high school level and develops
a mechanical teaching-evaluating device.   Finds that students
with low pre-program ability to sight-read rhythms showed
great improvement as a result of the program, while students
with high pre-program ability showed much less improvement.
The program was judged most effective as a remedial tool,
especially for students with little or no prior individual instruction.

414.   Trisman, Donald A.   <u>An Experimental Investigation of</u>
        <u>Maximal Speed Pacing Technique for Teaching Mu-</u>
        <u>sic Reading.</u>   Ph. D. dissertation, Cornell Univer-
        sity, 1964, 95 p. ;   LC 64-13,852;   DA XXVI/ 9,
        5253.
        The maximal speed pacing technique (subjects are
forced to respond at rates of speed which, for a given set of

stimuli, reach the limit of group capacity for correct response) was not demonstrated to be superior to the control
technique in the teaching of rhythmic reading to college students. The study used notation limited to flagged notes used
in vocal music. A by-product of this study was the development of a group test of rhythmic reading achievement with
established reliability and validity.
            Review by Alan H. Drake in Council for Research
in Music Education Bulletin, No. 13 (Spring 1968) 46-48.

414a. Wagner, Christoph; Ernst Piontek; and Ludwig
       Teckhaus. "Piano Learning and Programed In-
       struction." Journal of Research in Music Educa-
       tion, XXI/2 (Summer 1973) 106-22.
       Describes a method of programed instruction used
by the author to teach pianists tempo stability and precision
in performing rhythmic patterns consisting of equal durations
and patterns consisting of unequal durations. Experimental
data produced by time-interval measuring equipment coupled
to a Bechstein piano is fed into a Honeywell DDP-516 process
computer which can express readings of a pianist's tempo and
rhythm discrepancies in chart form, on punched cards, or on
a visual display unit. As well as being useful for directly
controlling the learning process, this apparatus may also be
used to obtain an objective picture of the pianist's long-range
development by means of regular tests.

415. Wiley, Charles A. An Experimental Study of Tachisto-
       scopic Techniques in Teaching Rhythmic Sight-
       Reading in Music. Ed. D. dissertation, University
       of Colorado, 1962, 265 p.; LC 63-2029; DA XXIII/
       10, 3925.
       Findings indicate that tachistoscopic techniques are
not significantly more effective than conventional techniques
as used in this study in the developing of rhythmic sight-
reading ability at the fifth grade level.

F. Instructional Materials

       Rhythm, an integral part of music, is necessarily
inherent in most vocal, instrumental, and ensemble methods
and studies of a general nature, however, only a representative sample of those which contain unusual or large sections
devoted to rhythmic instruction are included in this section.

Rather, the emphasis here is on the literature written specifically for rhythmic instruction, and while the following list in no way claims completeness, it does indicate the need for some good instructional materials which deal with contemporary rhythm.

Three types of instructional materials on rhythm are examined: 1) methods, 2) solfeggio, and 3) studies and etudes. The annotations give the educational level to which the material is suited, state the instrumentation for which it is published, contain brief descriptions of the contents, and cite any counting aids or unusual features which are used.

In the interest of providing easy access to the materials listed below, the current places of publication are furnished wherever possible. (For example, Belwin, Inc. recently merged with Mills Music, Inc. to become Belwin Mills Publishing Corp. and changed its address from Rockville Centre, NY to Melville, NY)

1.   Methods

Rhythm method books contain text, diagrams, and musical examples which isolate and explain rhythmic difficulties in an orderly sequence. The difficulties are then usually incorporated into short etudes or studies. The material is intended to be performed on a musical instrument.

Two theses which contain rhythm methods are also included in this section (see Feldman [No. 420] and Houseknecht [No. 423]). Methods useful for teaching contemporary rhythms include those by Creston (No. 417),

Leavitt (No. 426), and Rothman (Nos. 430, 431, and 432).

416.   Chapin, Jim.   Advanced Techniques for the Modern
         Drummer: Coordinated Independence as Applied
         to Jazz and Be-Bop.   New York: By the Author,
         50 Morningside Drive, 1948, reprinted in 1971,
         51 p.
         High school--college level.   One of the first books
on rhythmic independence.   Contains exercises which aim
"... to acquaint the drummer with some of the skills of
counterrhythmic [polyrhythmic] hand action."--p. 2.
         Includes pertinent discussion on the notation of jazz
rhythms and helpful instructional comments.

417.   Creston, Paul.   Rhythmicon.   New York: Franco
         Colombo, Inc.   Book I, 1964, pp. 1-20;   Book II,
         1964, pp. 21-42;   Book III, 1965, pp. 43-62.
         Other books in this series were unavailable for
         the present study.
         Elementary--college level.   A supplementary piano
method based upon the author's Principles of Rhythm (see
No. 37).
                    Rhythmicon is a practical dictionary of rhythms.
              Its main purpose is to present a clear concept
              of meters and rhythms through explanatory notes,
              practice drills and short pieces.... Books I
              through IV deal primarily with meters;   the
              books which follow take up the five rhythmic
              structures and polyrhythms.   (The five rhythmic
              structures are: 1. Regular Subdivision, 2. Ir-
              regular Subdivision, 3. Overlapping, 4. Regular
              Subdivision Overlapping and 5. Irregular Subdivi-
              sion Overlapping.)
                    With the introduction of each meter, explana-
              tory notes and practice drills are given before
              the short pieces.   The drills are technically as
              simple as possible, and the pieces are progres-
              sively graded....
                    The classic meters of 2/2, 3/2 and 6/4, and
              the rather common modern meters of 5/4 and
              5/8 are introduced in the first book in the event
              that the beginner is given simple pieces from
              these two periods. --Foreword, Book I.
                    Numbers and syllables are employed as counting
aids.

See also Creston's <u>Six Preludes</u>, Op. 38 for piano
(New York: Leeds Music Corp. , 1949, 16 p.).   These are
didactic pieces written as examples of the five rhythmic
structures.   They are analyzed by the composer in his article, "The Structure of Rhythm" (No. 38).

418.   Evans, Bob.   <u>Authentic Bongo Rhythms</u>.   New York:
          Henry Adler, Inc. , 1960;   copyright assigned 1966
          to Belwin Mills Publishing Corp. , Melville, NY,
          32 p.
          High school--college level.   Presents instructions,
pictures, and diagrams describing the basic technique of playing the bongo drums.   Gives definitions of musical terms
and signs, and explains note and rest values, meter signatures, the tumbao, and the cinquillo.   The main part of the
book illustrates the basic patterns for twenty-four Latin-
American rhythms as performed on the bongos.

419.   _____.   <u>Authentic Conga Rhythms</u>.   New York:
          Henry Adler, Inc. , 1960;   copyright assigned 1966
          to Belwin Mills Publishing Corp. , Melville, NY,
          32 p.
          A companion book to <u>Authentic Bongo Rhythms</u>
(No. 418).

420.   Feldman, Ivan W.   "The Rhythmic Approach to Band
          Playing. "   Unpublished M. M. thesis, De Paul Uni-
          versity, 1942, 53 p.
          Elementary--junior high school level.   Presents a
course of study to be used as a supplementary method for
band students who have had the equivalent of one year of elementary class instruction.   The course consists of original,
unison exercises stressing aspects of rhythm which, according to the author, are inadequately taught by existing band
methods.

      Findlay, Francis.   <u>Chrono-Rhythmics: Studies in
Rhythm Based upon Skeletal Rhythmic Design for the Mastery
of Rhythmic Timing</u>.   See No. 465.

421.   Gornston, David.   <u>Progressive Swing Readings</u>.   2
          vols.   New York: Gate Music Co. , 1944, 1956;
          copyright assigned 1970 to Sam Fox Publishing Co. ,
          Inc. , New York, 24 p. , 25 p.
          High school level.   Published for treble and bass
clef instruments.   Emphasis is on syncopation and the swing
style.   Arrows and numbers are employed as counting aids.

422. _____ and Harry Huffnagle. <u>Your Concert Reader.</u>
Boston: B. F. Wood Music Co., Inc., 1955, 24 p.
Junior high--high school level. Published for all
band and orchestral instruments. No score is published.
Comparisons of the same rhythms as notated in different
meters are made throughout the method, but the explanation
is left up to the teacher. Numbers, arrows, and syllables
are used as counting aids. Rhythmic variations on familiar
melodies are employed "... to prepare the instrumentalist
for the sight-reading of 'special' and 'trick' arrangements."--
p. 11. New material is introduced at a fast rate for this
level; no allowance is made for a slow beginner.

423. Houseknecht, Bruce H. "A Course of Study for the
Junior High School Band." Unpublished M. A. thesis, Eastman School of Music, University of
Rochester, 1943, 188 p.
Junior high school level. Maintains that the rhythmic content of existing junior high school band methods is
not given enough emphasis or repetititon to develop good sight
reading ability in students. Presents a course of study which
correlates the rhythmic unit content of 489 compositions from
five such band methods. The course contains numerous
examples of ten rhythmic units chosen for presentation and
aims to develop immediate and accurate responses to rhythmic notation.

424. Hudadoff, Igor. <u>Adventures in Rhythm.</u> Melville,
NY: Belwin Mills Publishing Corp., 1960, student's book 16 p., piano-conductor score 32 p.
Elementary--junior high school level. Published
for band instruments and conductor. Designed to develop the
recognition of groups of notes and rests as rhythmic patterns.
Patterns one measure in length are first presented individ-
ually and then incorporated into short phrases one line in
length. These may be played in unison or in harmony following the suggested chord progressions given. No instructional
comments or counting aids are included.

425. Leavitt, Joseph. <u>Reading by Recognition.</u> New York:
Henry Adler, Inc., 1963; copyright assigned 1966
to Belwin Mills Publishing Corp., Melville, NY,
40 p.
High school level. Published for snare drum.
Presents explanatory text and exercises for developing the
ability to "read by recognition." This term,
... simply defined, means that the musician

looks at a piece of music and plays it immediately because he recognizes it.   His brain has
stored away literally thousands of rhythms and
they are on tap for immediate application to the
instrument when the eye sees them. --p. 5.
Numbers and syllables are employed as counting
aids.

426. _____. The Rhythms of Contemporary Music.   New
         York: Henry Adler, Inc. , 1963; copyright assigned
         1966 to Belwin Mills Publishing Corp. , Melville,
         NY, 112 p.
         High school--college level.   Published as a percus-
sion method; also may serve as a "... rhythmic teaching
aid for all instruments" according to the author (p. 1).   The
text is divided in three parts: "I. The Most Common Time
Signatures," includes sections on counting, syncopation, and
music dictionaries; "II. Compound Triple and Quadruple
Time," includes a section on "abbreviated counting"; and
"III. Problems of the Professional in the Modern Repertoire,"
includes sections on ornaments (embellishments), repetition
studies, "artificial groups" (extrametrical rhythmic patterns),
etudes based on the works of modern composers, and excerpts
for percussion from the works of Woolen, Shostakovitch,
Antheil, Khatchaturian, Kabalevsky, Prokofiev, Serebrier,
Schuller, Ginastera, Cowell, and Stout.
         Numbers, syllables, and occasional ictus marks are
used as counting aids.   Explanatory text is included; however, the material is not self-instructional.

427. Mokrejs, John.   Lessons in Rhythm.   Chicago:
         Clayton F. Summy Co. , 1918, 29 p.
         High school level.   Assumes little knowledge of
rhythm at the start but progresses quickly and covers double-
dotted notes, sixty-fourth notes, and extrametrical subdivisions (patterns using subdivisions not normally implied in the
meter).   Although written primarily for piano students, the
book "... can be used by all students of music (vocal as well
as instrumental) and by simply playing the examples an octave higher or lower, they will fit any instrument."--Preface.
Note values are learned as characters of a phonetic alphabet
(1ABD, 2ABD, 3ABD, etc.).

428. Morello, Joe.   New Directions in Rhythm: Studies in
         3/4 and 5/4.   Chicago: Jomor Publications (sole
         agents: Ludwig Drum Co. , Chicago), 1963, 36 p.
         High school--college level.   Published for drums.

The purpose of this book is to develop freedom
and a natural feel for playing the odd time signatures [3/4 and 5/4] which have recently become
so popular in the jazz field. The ... exercises
are not just 'licks' to memorize and use indis-
criminately while working with a group, but constitute a systematic development of coordination
and a musical approach to playing in these different time signatures. --Preface.
Includes numerous musical examples showing how
rhythms in these meters are applied to actual performance.
The author has performed for many years with the Dave
Brubeck Quartet and has an international reputation.   The
text has the ring of true authenticity.

429. Raph, Alan. Dance Band Reading and Interpretation:
The Basic Concepts of Dance and Jazz Rhythms.
New York: Sam Fox Publishing Co. , Inc. , 1962,
44 p.
High school level.   Published for treble and bass
clef instruments.
The book's basic principle combines a group of
FIVE comprehensive rules (p. 3) to be learned
and applied to dance and jazz parts.   Many
examples of the most commonly used rhythms
are presented, explained, and used in context
with figures and etudes typical of actual dance
band music. --p. 2.
No counting aids are indicated in the music, but
the explanatory text and examples are exceptionally clear.
Review in Down Beat, XXXI (June 18, 1964) 34.

430. Rothman, Joel. Mixing Meters. Brooklyn, NY:
JR Publications, 251 E. 89th Street, 1964, 32 p.
Junior high-high school level.   This method is intended for percussionists but is applicable to other instruments.   According to the Foreword, the rhythms contained
in the exercises "... have been especially designed and presented in a developmental sequence for use by the beginning
student. "   The exercises consist of rhythmic patterns in
multimeter (changing or mixed meter) and ametrical notation
(without bar lines or meter signatures).   The patterns are
notated with stems and beams only--the note heads are miss-
ing.   This may cause quarter-note stems to be confused with
bar lines.   Notes are not spaced proportionately according to
their durational values.   Very few instructional comments or
counting aids are given.

431. _____. Pure Co-ordination for All Musicians (but
         Especially Drummers). Brooklyn, NY: JR Pub-
         lications, 251 E. 89th Street, 1967, 45 p.
         High school--college level. Dealing with poly-
rhythms, this book
              ... is designed to develop ... pure coordination,
              as opposed to coordination of one hand against
              the ride cymbal rhythm. In the exercises to
              develop pure coordination, one hand maintains a
              certain number of strokes at a steady and even
              pulsation, while the other hand maintains a dif-
              ferent number of strokes at the same tempo. --
              Preface.
         The book contains
              Exercises covering almost every conceivable
              combination of two rhythms, starting with one
              against two (1:2), and progressing through 1:3,
              1:4, etc. to 1:10. Then, starting with 2:3, the
              book moves through 2:4, 2:5 to 2:10, from 3:4
              through 3:10, and finally from 4:5 through 4:9. --
              from review in Instrumentalist, XXII/9 (Apr.
              1968) 16.

432. _____. Reading Can Be Odd: For the Beginner,
         Intermediate, and Professional Drummer. Brooklyn,
         NY: JR Publications, 251 E. 89th Street, 1963,
         58 p.
         High school level. Contains exercises consisting of
constantly changing rhythmic patterns written in 3/4, 5/4,
7/4, 3/8, 5/8, 7/8, 3/16, 5/16, and 7/16 meter. Very
few instructional comments are given. Numbers and syllables
are employed as counting aids.

433. Schaeffer, Don. A Systematic Approach to Reading
         Rhythms. Westbury, NY: Pro Art Publications,
         Inc. , 1967, 24 p.
         Elementary level. Published for trumpet, clarinet,
and horn. Designed to be used as a supplement to any
method. Emphasis is placed on rhythmic fundamentals,
dynamics, and articulation. All new materials are presented
at the beginning of each exercise and are marked with numbers and arrows. Tempo indications are explained as they
are introduced.

434. Shaughnessy, Ed. The New Time Signatures in Jazz
         Drumming. New York: Henry Adler, Inc. , 1966;
         copyright assigned 1966 to Belwin Mills Publishing

Corp., Melville, NY, 39 p.
High school--college level. The book is devoted to
the use of 3/4, 5/4, and 7/4 meters in the modern jazz
style and emphasizes developing the "swing" of these meters
on the full drum set. Provides practical rhythmic patterns,
advice on jazz interpretation and conception, and instructions
on how to analyze and interpret a modern drum arrangement
using these meters.

435. Skornicka, Joseph E. Boosey & Hawkes Instrumental
       Course: B^b Cornet or Trumpet. Part I. New
       York: Boosey & Hawkes, Inc., 1946, 48 p.
       Elementary level. Published for all band instru-
ments and piano-conductor score. Although designed as a
general method, its unique approach to rhythm is cause for
inclusion here. After one long tone exercise to develop
breathing, the quarter note is introduced. The various note
values are presented on the basis of the quarter note and
multiples thereof, i. e., the half note is called a "2 quarter
note," the dotted half a "3 quarter note," and the whole note
a "4 quarter note." Little use is made of numbers and syllables.
       See also No. 256, Joseph E. Skornicka, The Func-
tion of Time and Rhythm in Instrumental Music Reading Com-
petency.
       See also Joseph Skornicka and Joseph Bergeim,
Boosey & Hawkes Band Method (New York: Boosey & Hawkes,
Inc., 1947) and R. Moehlmann and J. E. Skornicka, Instrumental Course for Strings (New York: Boosey & Hawkes,
Inc.).

436. Spear, Sammy; Robert Stein; and Nicholas Lamitola.
       Basic Syncopation: A Practical Approach to Stage
       Band Reading, Interpretation, and Articulation.
       Westbury, NY: Pro Art Publications, Inc., 1967,
       56 p.
       High school level. Published for trumpet, saxo-
phone, and trombone. Contains twenty-six lessons which
stress interpretation and articulation of rhythm in both the
"classical" and "popular" styles. Arrows and syllables are
employed as counting aids.

437. Teal, Larry. Studies in Time Division: A Practical
       Approach to Accurate Rhythm Perception. Ann
       Arbor, MI: University Music Press, 1959, 24 p.
       High school level. Published in "the playable range
of all treble clef instruments." Contains short exercises and

studies first to be recited using numbers, syllables, and a
pencil or hand tap, and then to be played on an instrument.
This book is unique in that it derives all durational note
values from the sixteenth note and its expansion.

2. Solfeggio

Solfeggio books devoted to the study of rhythm usually employ a system of rhythmic syllabization or counting,
often coupled with conducting patterns or other rhythmic movement. The goal of this type of book is to develop the student's understanding of rhythm and his ability to translate
rhythm syllables or notation into perceivable sound when necessary. All the elements of the rhythm method book are
present, except that the material in the solfeggio book is
usually not intended to be played on musical instruments,
although this would serve a useful educational purpose.

After examining nearly fifty books on theory, sight
singing, and solfeggio, the following items have been selected
as being especially useful for rhythmic instruction. They
range in date from Bona's Rhythmical Articulation: ... (No.
438), first Italian edition published in 1897, to Phillips' The
Rhythm Book: ... (No. 449), published in 1971. For material especially valuable for teaching contemporary rhythm,
see Hindemith (No. 441), Jersild (No. 443), Phillips (No.
449), Starer (No. 452), and Thomson (No. 453).

438.   Bona, Pasquale. Rhythmical Articulation: A Complete
        Method. Translated from the 4th Italian ed. , rev.
        and augmented by the author, by Theodore Baker.
        New York: G. Schirmer, Inc. , 1925, 72 p. (First
        Italian ed. published in 1897.)
        Junior high school--college level. A collection of
studies progressively arranged and divided in three sections.
Sparse instructional comments are given, and, except for
numbers indicated above the notes on page one, virtually no

counting aids are included. The student is to pronounce the
name of each note using solmization. The rhythms become
quite complicated and varied by the end of the book, and the
range covered is over two octaves.
    See also Pasquale Bona, Rhythmical Articulation,
Parts II and III, selected and transcribed by William Fitch
for bass clef instruments (New York: Carl Fischer, Inc. ,
1969, 47 p.) and its review by John Christie in Instrumentalist, XXIV/10 (May 1970) 24.

439. Britton, Mervin W. Rhythm in Performance. Tempe,
      AZ: By the Author, Music Department, Arizona
      State University, 1960, 64 p. (Dittoed.)
      High school--college level. The book's purpose, as
stated in the Introduction, is to help the reader build a solid
foundation for rhythmic performance and to further his ability
to understand, interpret, and define the terms and symbols of
notation. Offers two general rules for accurate rhythmic performance:
      1. When possible, count units which are one
      half the duration of the units to be performed,
      or equal to the smallest unit to be performed.
      2. When possible, prepare (perform mentally)
      the rhythm pattern at least one basic beat before
      it is performed. --p. 13.
      Contains helpful, instructional text with non-pitched
exercises for counting and conducting rhythms in "simple,"
"compound," "complex," and "changing" meters. Conducting
patterns, numbers, and syllables are used as counting aids.
Supplementary assignments designed to improve notational
skills, rhythmic dictation exercises, and a three-page glossary of terms are included.
      See also No. 194, Mervin W. Britton, "A New
Philosophy to Teaching Rhythm. "

440. Dumm, James. Rhythm Manual of Basic Rhythmic
      Exercises. Rochester, NY: By the Author, 35
      Holly Ridge Circle, 1965, 17 p.
      Elementary--high school level. Contains nineteen
groups of exercises organized in a progressive manner. The
rhythms are to be sung using the syllable "ta" while clapping
the pulse. Instructive comments include an excellent discussion and musical examples of sustaining notes for their full
duration. Special sections are devoted to the tie, dotted
notes, and triplets. Two sections contain difficult rhythmic
patterns found in music often performed by high school orchestras.

Findlay, Francis. Chrono-Rhythmics: Studies in
Rhythm Based upon Skeletal Rhythmic Design for the Mastery
of Rhythmic Timing. See No. 465.

441. Hindemith, Paul. Elementary Training for Musicians.
      2nd ed. rev. New York: Schott Music Corp.
      (Sole agents: Belwin Mills Publishing Corp.,
      Melville, NY), 1949, 237 p.
      High school--college level. Written by a distin-
guished composer and educator, this text has enjoyed widespread use in theory and solfeggio courses since its publication. It is included here for its emphasis on the sight reading, ear training, and notation of rhythm and meter.
            Each chapter of the book is divided into three
            sections, A. Action in Time; B. Action in
            Space; C. Coordinated Action. The first sec-
            tion contains exercises in Rhythm and Meter,
            both in their basic forms.... Action in Space
            comprises instruction about pitch, intervals,
            and scales, which in Coordinated Action is com-
            bined with the rhythmic and metric experiences
            of the first section.... Interspersed in all three
            sections are complete courses in Notation and
            Dictation. --Preface, p. xii.
      The book is intended for use in a class situation;
its aim is to promote musical activity for the teacher as well
as the student. According to the author (p. xi), the text is
too difficult for the average student to understand, obliging
the teacher to offer more complete explanations. The rhythmic exercises are to be sung on "la" or played while tapping
or clapping the pulse or variations of the pulse, indicated by
small notes beneath most of the exercises. The chapters
progress in an orderly manner from simple to complex and
discuss metric accents, conducting patterns, syncopation,
"Triplets and Other Divisions by Factors Not Implied in the
Time-Signatures" (extrametrical patterns), quintuple and septuple meters, and indications for changing tempi.

442. Hudadoff, Igor. Just for Counting: A Method to Teach
      Rhythm for All Instruments and Voices. Melville,
      NY: Belwin Mills Publishing Corp., 1957, 31 p.
      Elementary level; assumes no previous musical
knowledge. Uses familiar melodies to illustrate each rhythmic pattern. The rhythms are notated on a two-lined staff
and the melody is included on a separate staff beneath this.
Basic theory, durational values, and definitions of terms are
given. The student is required to count aloud, tap with his

foot, and clap the beginning of each note. Numbers, syllables, and arrows are used as counting aids. Instructional comments are included; however, the book is intended to be used with the help of a teacher.

443. Jersild, Jörgen. Ear Training: Basic Instruction in Melody and Rhythm Reading. Translated by Gerd Schiötz. Book II: Rhythm Reading. Copenhagen: Wilhelm Hansen (sole agents: G. Schirmer, Inc., New York), 1951, 80 p.
College level. This thorough text is concerned with "... the theoretical instruction of the serious music student ... in conservatories, universities, music schools, etc."-- Book I, Preface, p. 5. In the prefaces to both books, the author, a professor at the Royal Danish Conservatory of Music in Copenhagen, offers the philosophy of his approach and suggests procedures for using the text to teach less advanced students and for self-instruction.
Book II: Rhythm Reading is aimed at training the student to read rhythms and at developing precision in performance. It is organized in a progressive manner, from simple to complex, and covers "quadruple and duple" (binary), "triple and compound" (ternary), and "shifting meters" (multimeter), as well as quintuple and septuple meters. Chapter V, "Concerning Tempo," gives unique and valuable ideas on using an ordinary wrist watch to deduce accurate tempi. Memorizing the metronomical markings of familiar pieces is suggested as an aid in reproducing the tempi of unfamiliar music. The text includes illustrations from music literature and is supplemented by a series of preliminary drills and exercises. These are to be either articulated on some neutral syllable or combined with stepwise melodic material and sung accompanied by beating the appropriate pulse. Supplementary elementary reading exercises in one-line notation are included.
Review by Sherwood E. Hall in Music Educators Journal, LIV/2 (Oct. 1967) 80-84; Roy Jesson in Musical Times, CVIII/1494 (Aug. 1967) 709; Victor Payne in Music in Education, XXXI/325 (May-June 1967) 472.

444. Jordon, Helen H. Meter and Rhythm. Modern Musicianship Series. [New York]: By the Author, [111 W. 57th Street], 1948, 196 p.
Elementary--junior high school level. Preliminary definitions and explanatory comments are given on conducting patterns, major scale construction, music symbols, meter, and rhythm. The remainder of the book consists of ninety groups of non-pitched rhythm exercises which progress in

small steps from simple to complex and cover rhythmic patterns in "simple" (binary) duple, triple, and quadruple meters
notated with the eighth, quarter, and half note as the pulse.
The student is to sing the rhythms in scale patterns to the
syllables "do, re, mi," etc. while conducting the meter. All
exercises (as many as twelve) in each group are placed on the
page with their corresponding pulses vertically aligned and the
notes spaced proportionately. Phrase marks are included.
         See also Helen H. Jordon, Advanced Meter and
Rhythm, Modern Musicianship Series ([New York]: By the
Author, [111 W. 57th Street], 1948), a companion volume to
Meter and Rhythm, containing rhythmic exercises in "compound" (ternary) meters.

445. Langenus, Gustave. Rhythm-Builder. Port Washington,
         NY: Ensemble Music Press (Sole agents: C.
         Fischer, Inc. , New York), 1933, 20 p.

446. Lenom, Clément. Rhythm by Solfeggio: A Practical
         Method for the Development of the Sense of Time
         and of Rhythm. New York: Coleman-Ross Co. ,
         Inc. , 1944, 137 p.
         High school--college level. This text was used for
many years by the author in his solfeggio classes at the New
England Conservatory of Music. It contains explanatory comments and 405 exercises presenting basic patterns in binary
and ternary duple, triple, and quadruple meters. Seven pages
are devoted to syncopation. The extrametrical patterns
covered are limited to duplets, triplets, quadruplets, and
sextuplets; quintuplets and septuplets are not treated.
         The student is to perform the exercises by naming
the notes in rhythm, using the syllables "do, re, mi," etc.
(but not by singing the actual pitches), while conducting the
meter according to given conducting patterns. The method of
counting rests and the illogical and awkward conducting patterns which are suggested, although not unusual for such
texts at the time this text was published, might confuse today's students using the text without a teacher's guidance.

447. Lockwood, William D. The Music Rhythm Teaching
         Series. Valhalla, NY: Stanley Bowmar Co. ,
         Inc. , 1962. Two sets of Select-O-Cards, Select-
         O-Needle, and instruction book.
         Elementary level. The selection of cards to teach
specific rhythms is accomplished by inserting the select-o-
needle through certain holes in the cards. A great many
combinations of rhythmic patterns are possible by rearranging

the cards. Students are to count the pulse and clap the
rhythms. Numbers and syllables are used as counting aids.

448. McHose, Allen I. and Ruth N. Tibbs. Sight-Singing
      Manual. 2nd ed. New York: Appleton-Century-
      Crofts, Inc., 1945, 105 p.
      College level. Included because of its organization
emphasizing the rhythmic aspect of music and the influence
its system of rhythmic syllables has had on other texts and
methods. Contains 350 short melodies, from one to seven
lines in length, chosen from 18th- to 20th-century music
literature. These may be studied applying pitch or rhythmic
syllables; however, no explanation of pitch problems is
given. A brief explanation with suggested rhythmic syllables
and conducting patterns precedes each section dealing with
new rhythmic problems. Various subjects covered include
"Elementary Problems in Rhythm," "unequal Time Durations
in Compound Rhythm," "Subdivision of the Simple Beat," "The
Tie," "Syncopation," "Superimposed Backgrounds and Superimposed Meter," "Subdivision of the Background," "The Divided Beat," and "Less Common Meter Signatures and Mixed
Meters." The Introduction (p. 5) presents two rules for the
rhythmic interpretation of the appogiatura.

449. Phillips, Peter. The Rhythm Book: Studies in Rhyth-
      mic Reading and Principles. New York: Associated
      Music Publishers, Inc., 1971, 201 p.
      Junior high school--college level. The text's pur-
pose is to give a comprehensive grasp of the principles of
rhythmic performance, notation, and theory. A tripartite
approach is used: 1) the rhythmic aspect under consideration
is presented by explanatory text, diagrams, and musical examples; 2) it is then used in rhythmic drills in which the
student is to tap the pulse with his hand according to ictus
marks provided in the music while intoning the rhythms on
the syllable "ta"; and 3) related examples (including two com-
posed by the author) selected from 11th- to 20th-century music literature are incorporated into the text and are to be
sung or played by the student.
      The book begins with basic studies covering note
and rest durational values and proceeds with major sections
on "Simple Time" and "Compound Time" to a consideration of
"Combinations of Basic Beat and Metric Types," which includes hemiola, triplets, duplets, and "changing" and "additive" meters. Seven pages devoted to basic conducting technique discuss the conductor's function, basic gestures, and
the downbeat and gives French and German conducting patterns.

The appendixes include suggested procedures and preliminary studies for sight singing, "A [ten page] Guide to the Principles of Rhythmic Notation" prepared with the assistance of Ronald Herder, composer and editor-in chief of Associated Music Publishers, Inc., "A Chart of Quintuple Meters," "Five-, Six- and Nine-Beat Conducting Patterns," "Some Observations on Compound Meter Signatures," "Tempo Markings in English, Italian, German and French," a list of the sources of the musical examples, and an alphabetized listing of footnotes by subject.

450. Rossi, Giosue. The Master Method of Rhythmical Articulation. Elmhurst, NY: By the Author, 40-34 Junction Blvd., 1926, 100 p.
        High school--college level. The text, written in English and Italian, is organized in three parts: Part I, "Principles of Music," presents definitions and explanations of terms, symbols, durational values of notes and rests, meter signatures, and basic music theory; Part II, "Rhythmical Division of the Figures," includes solfeggio exercises employing the tie, dot, double dot, embellishments or grace notes, and numerous other rhythmic patterns in binary and ternary duple, triple, and quadruple meter; Part III, "Solfeggio," very briefly covers transposition and 5/4 and 7/4 meter and contains a six-page dictionary of musical terms.
        The student is to pronounce the rhythms of the examples using the syllables "do, re, mi," etc. while conducting the meter using the given conducting patterns. The suggested method for counting rests and the conducting patterns are similar to those used in Lenom's Rhythm by Solfeggio: ... (No. 446).

451. Rothman, Joel. Teaching Rhythm. Brooklyn, NY: JR Publications, 251 E. 89th Street, 1967, 80 p.
        Junior high--senior high school level. The book
        ... was written for the express purpose of teaching rhythm as a separate entity to all instrumentalists, whether it be in a class situation or during private instruction; the reader is merely expected to clap each exercise. --Preface.
        Provides an extremely thorough presentation of twenty-three rhythmic patterns, proceeds at a very slow rate, and gives plenty of practice material. Starts with quarter notes and concludes with extrametrical patterns such as sixteenth-note triplets within eighth-note triplets. Numbers and syllables are employed as counting aids.
        Review in Instrumentalist, XXII/9 (Apr. 1968) 16.

452. Starer, Robert. Rhythmic Training. New York: MCA
      Music, Inc., 1969, 84 p.
      High school--college level. The author, a composer
and faculty member of the Juilliard School of Music, has con-
cluded "... that inadequate grasp of rhythmic patterns is often
the cause of poor sight-reading...." and "... that lack of
familiarity with 5 and 7 time and changing meters, particularly in the early stages of musical training, has contributed
much to the unjustified fears of performing 20th-century music."--Preface.
      Essentially, the writer agrees with the statements
made in the following review:
      The book contains 100 exercises progressing
      from simple to complex. Each chapter intro-
      duces a specific rhythmic situation then gives
      exercises dealing with this particular situation.
      The number of exercises in each chapter is de-
      signed to meet the needs of the average student
      . . . .
      Each exercise consists of two lines. The up-
      per line represents the rhythm, the lower line
      the pulse. The author suggests that the student
      perform the upper line by singing, humming, or
      speaking on a neutral syllable and at the same
      time tap with the hand or foot or conduct the
      lower line.... The drills begin with the more
      common rhythmic divisions, such as dividing the
      beat into two, three, or four equal parts then
      progress to mixing divisions of the beat, dividing
      the beat into five and seven equal parts, changing
      the rate of pulse, and polyrhythms.--from review
      in Instrumentalist, XXIV/10 (May 1970) 20-21.
      The text includes some of the evolving practices of
modern rhythmic notation, such as the double-figure method
of expressing extrametrical subdivisions, e. g., $\overset{2:3}{\prod}$ for $\overset{2}{\prod}$
and $\overset{4:3}{\prod}$ for $\overset{4}{\prod}$ (p. 44) and the extension of beams
over or under rests to give the visual effect of all the notes
being present within a beamed group, e. g., $\overset{3}{\prod}$ for $\overset{3}{\prod}$
and $\overset{3}{\prod}$ for $\overset{3}{\prod}$ (p. 84).

      Teal, Larry. Studies in Time Division: A Practical
Approach to Accurate Rhythm Perception. See No. 437.

453. Thomson, William. Advanced Music Reading. Bel-
      mont, CA: Wadsworth Publishing Co. , Inc. ,
      1969, 245 p.
        College level. Included here for Chapter VI,
"Rhythmic Problems," which contains explanatory text, suggested mnemonic aids, and numerous musical examples "from
the literature" covering the areas indicated by the chapter
subtitles: "Changing Meters," "Composite Meters," "Difficult Subdivisions of the Basic Duration," and "Irregular Divisions of the Basic Duration." The musical examples (some
are a page in length) are identified by composer or country
of origin; specific titles are given only occasionally. The
student is instructed to "sing" the examples, presumably on
a neutral syllable. Counting aids are not indicated in the
examples, but the section on composite meters contains a
valuable explanation of short and long pulses.
        See also William Thomson, Introduction to Music
Reading: Concepts and Applications (Belmont, CA: Wads-
worth Publishing Co. , Inc. , 1966, 260 p.), the prerequisite
book to Advanced Music Reading.

454. Wedge, George A. Rhythm in Music: A Textbook.
      New York: G. Schirmer, Inc. , 1927, 54 p.
        Elementary--junior high school level. Contains an
exposition of the theory of rhythm supplemented by thirty-
seven practical drills. The book aims to develop the student's feeling for rhythm by correlating the fundamental principles of rhythm with the development of a muscular technique
using the strict pulse of walking and a combination of poetry
reading and counting.

                    3. Studies and Etudes

        Rhythm study and etude books contain pieces de-

signed to aid the instrumentalist in developing certain aspects

of his rhythmic performance ability. Each study or etude is

usually devoted to one or two rhythmic difficulties and is one

or two pages in length. Often, brief explanatory text is in-

cluded; however, it is of secondary importance.

        For material particularly useful for teaching con-

temporary rhythm see Blazevich (No. 457), Cirone (No. 458),

Dufresne (No. 462), Gates (No. 467), Musser and Del Borgo

(No. 473), Nagel (No. 474), and Ostrander (No. 475).

455. Allard, Joe. Advanced Rhythms. New York: Charles
     Colin, 1968, 1972, 46 p.
        High school--college level. Published for treble
clef instruments. Contains 134 four-line rhythmical exercises
in the modern jazz style. No instructional comments or
counting aids are given, so the instructor should be experienced in the modern jazz style. Key signatures up to five
flats and six sharps are used; chord symbols are included.

456. Bellson, Louis and Gil Breines. Modern Reading Text
     in 4/4. New York: Henry Adler, Inc., 1963;
     copyright assigned 1966 to Belwin Mills Publishing
     Corp., Melville, NY, 91 p.
        High school--college level. The cover states that
the book is intended "for all instruments," but the notation is
on one pitch as in snare drum methods.
        The object of this text is to acquaint the reading
        Musician with the most comprehensive and popu-
        lar methods of notating syncopated rhythms used
        in all forms of music. (i.e., Jazz, Clas-
        sical, Latin, Show, Dance Bands, etc.)--Preface.
The studies are arranged progressively and become
fairly difficult by the end of the book. A two-page preface
discusses interpretation of the "Jazz Feel."

457. Blazevich, Vladimir. Rhythmical Sequences. Trans-
     scribed by Alfred H. Hicks. New York: Omega
     Music Edition (sole agents: Sam Fox Publishing
     Co., Inc., New York), 1954, 31 p.
        College level. Published for clarinet and trumpet;
also available in its original form as Twenty-Six Sequences
for trombone. Contains twenty-six studies in binary form.
Both parts of each study present a rhythmical idea one phrase
in length which is repeated in a stepwise sequence. No instructional comments or counting aids are given. Includes
difficult rhythmic patterns, regular and irregular subdivision
of the measure, multimeter, metrical sequence, syncopation,
and meters such as 5/2, 5/4, 7/4, and 11/4. The interest
and challenge one feels while playing the initial statement of
the rhythmical idea in each study tends to turn quickly to
boredom as the rhythm and its melody are stated in sequence
seven more times. Nevertheless, the material repays careful
study.

        Bona, Pasquale. Rhythmical Articulation: A Complete
Method. See No. 438.

458. Cirone, Anthony J. Portraits in Rhythm. Melville,

NY: Belwin Mills Publishing Corp., 1966, 54 p.
College level. An excellent and attractively en-
graved book of fifty studies for snare drum.
          ... form has been emphasized throughout this
          text: in the first section by pointing out themes,
          and any reworking processes they may undergo;
          in the second section by basing studies on vari-
          ous classical structures, which are fully explained
          before each exercise; in the third section in a
          manner similar to the first, but with more in-
          volved exercises. 'Unusual' meters, shifting
          bar-lines, and irregular phrases are used
          throughout this manual, ... --Foreword.
The studies contain multimeter (changing meter);
study No. 34 employs metrical sequence (constantly alternating 3/8 and 2/8 meter).

459. Colin, Charles. Thirty-Five Original Studies in Mod-
       ern Rhythms. New York: Charles Colin, 1972,
       24 p.
       High school level. Published for "all" instruments.
Studies are attractive melodically as well as rhythmically.
Each concentrates on one or two syncopated patterns in the
jazz style and is accompanied by explanatory comments. No
counting aids are given.

460. _____ and "Bugs" [Maurice] Bower. Rhythms.
       2 vols. in 1. New York: Charles Colin, 1950,
       1958, 1972, 47 p.
       One of the most thorough books available on the
junior high--high school level. Published for "all" instruments. Contains 242 short studies dealing with twenty-six
syncopated patterns. The patterns are shown as being derived from constituent, tied eighth notes. Arrows are employed as counting aids. Contains no text or instructional
comments. The material may be played according to strict
or swing style.
       See also Charles Colin and "Bugs" [Maurice]
Bower, Rhythms for Modern Concert Band (New York:
Charles Colin, 1966).

461. _____ and Grover C. Yaus. Easy Steps to Rhythm.
       New York: Charles Colin, 1959, 20 p.
       Elementary--junior high school level. Published in
unison for all band instruments except those pitched in F;
no score is published. Contains ninety-six exercises in
scale form; all are within the range of an octave.

Especially valuable to the beginner as the first
thirteen exercises are within the interval of a
second; the first forty exercises do not exceed
the interval of a sixth. --Foreword.
Arrows, numbers, and syllables are used as counting aids. New rhythmic patterns are introduced at a rate
slightly slower than normal.

462. Dufresne, Gaston. Develop Sight Reading. Edited by
      Roger Voisin. New York: Charles Colin, 1954,
      59 p.
      High school--college level. Published for treble
and bass clef instruments. Transcribed for snare drum by
G. David Peter. Contains fifty-four studies incorporating
frequent changes of metrical and extrametrical rhythmic patterns, syncopation, multimeter, and meters such as 3/1,
5/4, 5/8, 7/8, 11/8, and 17/16. Brief comments warning
of probable rhythmic difficulties are included for the studies
in the second half of the book.

463. Dunham, Sonny. Advanced Course in Swing Rhythms.
      New York: Robbins Music Corp. (sole agents:
      Big Three Music Corp., New York), 1937, 32 p.
      High school--college level. Published for trumpet
and trombone. Contains sixty-two studies, one-half page in
length, dealing with syncopated patterns (some are quite extended). Most studies include brief instructional comments.
Arrows are used as counting aids.

464. Endsley, Gerald. Odd Meter Etudes for Trumpet.
      Vol. I. Denver, CO: Tromba Publications,
      1971, 14 p.
      Junior high--high school level. A rather amateurish
contribution to the beginning trumpeter's study repertory.
Contains scales, etudes (called exercises in the body of the
book), and two duets written in 5/4, 7/4, 5/8, 7/8, and
multimeter. The use of non-standard notation, misspelled
words, and incorrect rhythms and notation places a limited
value on the book.

465. Findlay, Francis. Chrono-Rhythmics: Studies in
      Rhythm Based upon Skeletal Rhythmic Design for
      the Mastery of Rhythmic Timing. New York:
      Sprague-Coleman, 1939, 62 p.
      High school--college level. Most of the studies
are written in two voices using the treble and bass clefs.
They are intended to be played on an instrument (most

practicably on a keyboard instrument), "... but when no instrument is available they can be studied with profit by beating the measure and tapping, or pulsating the voice, ...
while singing or 'ta-ta-ing' the figuration."--p. 19.
    Contains eighteen progressively arranged groups of
rhythmic studies a few measures to two lines in length.
Stresses developing the ability to perceive various architectonic levels of rhythm.   Skeletal rhythmic patterns (note
stems and beams without the note heads) are indicated between the staves to clarify the inner structure of the studies.
Extensive text is devoted to explanations of rhythmic notation
and suggestions on how to use the book.   Syncopation, polyrhythm, and extrametrical and anacrustic rhythmic patterns
are included.

466.   Gates, Everett. Odd Meter Duets. New York: Gate
       Music Co. , 1964; copyright assigned 1970 to Sam
       Fox Publishing Co. , Inc. , New York, 24 p.
         Junior high--high school level.   Published for tre-
ble clef instruments.   These sixteen duets are useful as an
introduction to the study of the author's Odd Meter Etudes
(No. 467) and of contemporary music in general.
              The harmonies which are implied or outlined in
              these duets are based almost entirely on stylistic
              elements found in the music of the 'period of
              common practice' and not on contemporary prac-
              tice.   The problems presented are primarily
              those of meter and rhythm.   A wide variety of
              forms are utilized, as well as many types of
              musical treatment, such as canonic imitation,
              free obbligato, contrary motion, progressive
              development of melodic 'cells', thematic develop-
              ment and variation, ostinato, etc. --Foreword.
         Short comments on the melodic, harmonic, rhyth-
mic, and formal structure of the duets are included in the
table of contents.   The ranges are restricted to make the
material practical for a great variety of instruments.

467.   _____. Odd Meter Etudes. New York: David
       Gornston, 1962; copyright assigned 1970 to Sam
       Fox Publishing Co. , Inc. , New York, 24 p.
         High school--college level.   Published for treble
clef instruments.
              This is a collection of 21 études (original and
              excerpts) plus 2 pages of helpful examples for
              scale exercises in odd rhythms.   The book is
              a 'must' as a supplement to intermediate studies

for specific instruments.... This excellent book
meets odd metric problems head on but in a
thoroughly understandable and playable fashion.
In addition the études employ good examples of
structural patterns and unusual scales including
one with twelve-tone treatment. Salient features
are pointed out in brief remarks at the bottom
of each page. All in all a very superior book.
--Review by Harwood Simmons in New York
State School Music News, XXV/9 (May-June
1962) 21.

468. Huffnagle, Harry. Rhythm Duets. New York: David
Gornston, 1948, 1950; copyright assigned 1970 to
Sam Fox Publishing Co., Inc., New York, 16 p.
Junior high--high school level. Published for two
saxophones, clarinets, or violins. Contains nine duets em-
ploying syncopation.

469. _____ and David Gornston. Melody Way to Syncopation. New York: David Gornston, 1957; copyright
assigned 1970 to Sam Fox Publishing Co., Inc.,
New York, 24 p.
High school level. Published for all band instruments with piano-conductor score. Contains five pages of
explanatory examples comparing syncopated patterns as notated in different meters and twenty studies employing syncopation. Arrows, numbers, and syllables are employed as
counting aids. Includes quarter-note triplets and hemiola.

470. Hyman, Dick. Duets in Odd Meters and Far-Out
Rhythms. [n. p.]: Eastlake Music, Inc. (sole
agents: Cimino Publications, Inc., Westbury,
NY), 1965, 25 p.
Junior high--high school level. Published for treble clef instruments. A graded series of sixteen duets employing such meters as 5/8, 7/8, and 15/8, irregular subdivision of the measure, and multimeter. The range is
limited, making the material playable on a great many instruments.

471. McLeod, James "Red" and Norman Staska. Rhythm
Etudes. Minneapolis, MN: Schmitt, Hall &
McCreary Co., 1966, 33 p.
Junior high--high school level. Published for all
band instruments with condensed score. The material is ar-
ranged in sixteen progressive units, each encompassing a

given meter signature and a variety of keys. Each unit contains several chord progressions to which a number of suggested rhythm patterns may be played, and several short
rhythm studies. Some units contain exercises using ties and
"rhythmic displacement," and songs arranged for full band.
A unique feature is that exercises of varying degrees of difficulty may be performed simultaneously at the teacher's dis-
cretion in order to develop harmonic and rhythmic independence. One page is devoted to 5/4 and 7/4 meter; syncopation is covered by four pages on "dance style."
        Numbers, syllables, and the foot tap are used as
counting aids. Supplementary instructional comments on basic
articulations, improvisation, and dance style interpretation
are included at the end of the book. Two additional pages
of teaching suggestions are included in the conductor's
book.

472.   Morales, Humberto and Henry Adler. How to Play
        Latin American Rhythm Instruments. Supplementary
        section by Ubaldo Nieto. Edited by F. Henri Klick-
        mann. New York: Henry Adler, Inc., 1954; copy-
        right assigned 1966 to Belwin Mills Publishing Corp.,
        Melville, NY, 132 p.
        Junior high school--college level. "... contains a
series of exercises especially written for Latin-American Instruments, together with numerous illustrations showing the
correct method of playing these instruments."--Foreword.
Includes full percussion scores of over twenty Latin-American
rhythms, with text in English and Spanish.

473.   Musser, Willard I. and Elliot Del Borgo. The Rhythm
        of Contemporary Music: A Collection of Melodious
        Studies Which Progressively Explore the Rhythmic
        Concepts of 20th Century Music. Port Washington,
        NY: Alfred Music Co., Inc., 1971, 32 p.
        An excellent book of studies for the junior high--
high school level. Published for treble clef instruments.
        ... [It] is designed to teach and familiarize stu-
        dents with the rhythmic meters, various stressed
        accentuations, as well as rhythmic structures so
        often found in contemporary music, but not ne-
        cessarily introduced in the many fine method
        books. These etudes were conceived to develop
        the student's knowledge of music while also de-
        veloping his technical proficiency through ma-
        terial in a range which should not be taxing or
        fatiguing. --p. 1.
Few accidentals and easy key signatures are used;

harmonic implications are mostly common practice period. The
book is divided in two sections, the first containing material
similar to but easier than the second. A selection from the
table of contents indicates the material covered: "Changing
Time Signatures," "Five And Seven Beat Measures," "Changes
In Pulse-Groups Without Signature Alterations," "Unlike Beat
Divisions," "Unlike Beat Divisions With Change Of Time Signa-
tures," "Changes Of Compound Meter To Quarter Note Units,"
"The Quarter Note Triplet," "Beat Units Containing Five Notes,"
"Five and Various Threes," "Changes Of Meter With Eighth-
Note Remaining Constant," "Changes of Meter With a Specific
Note Value Remaining Constant," and "The Five-Eight And
Three-Eight Changes." Brief instructional comments and sug-
gestions accompany each of the above topics. A glossary of
terms used in the book is included.

474. Nagel, Robert. Rhythmic Studies: Articulation Drills
      and Concert Duets for Developing Rhythmic Tech-
      nique in Conception and Execution. Hempstead,
      NY: Mentor Music, Inc. (sole agents: Sam Fox
      Publishing Co. , Inc. , New York), 1968, 40 p.
      College level. Published separately for trumpet
and trombone. This is one of the few books containing study
material comparable in metric and rhythmic structure to 20th-
century music. Seven groups of articulation drills and eight
concert duets include various unusual and irregular groupings,
multimeter, regular and irregular subdivision of the measure,
and "rhythmic modulation" (metric modulation). One page of
study notes is provided. The duets can also be played by
trumpet and trombone, each using its own book.
      Review by Mary Rasmussen in Brass and Woodwind
Quarterly, II/1 & 2 (Spring-Summer 1969) 71.

475. Ostrander, Allen. Shifting Meter Studies for Bass
      Trombone or Tuba. North Easton, MA: Robert
      King Music Co. , 1965, 20 p.
      College level. Contains nineteen studies employing
shifting meters (multimeter) and irregular subdivision of the
measure (such as a 9/8 measure divided into four unequal
beats). Includes a chart of suggested slide positions for the
bass trombone with a double valve in F and "flatted" E.
Trombonists with a single valve bass trombone must adjust
their valve to E or "flatted" E to play the studies. Four of
the studies have brief instructional comments pertaining to
the rhythmic aspects of the music. Study No. 11 is written
in two ways, comparing what the author terms "classical"
and "dance" notation. Some of the studies use non-standard
rhythmic notation, making it necessary for most students to

add ictus marks to the music in order to delineate the beats.
Review by Mary Rasmussen in Brass and Woodwind
Quarterly, II/1 & 2 (Spring-Summer 1969) 75.

476. Paisner, Ben. Nineteen Swing Etudes. Enlarged edi-
      tion. New York: David Gornston, 1944, 1967;
      copyright assigned 1970 to Sam Fox Publishing Co.,
      Inc., New York, 28 p.
      High school level. Published for treble and bass
clef instruments. Contains twenty-three studies, some two
or three pages in length, with general comments on style and
interpretation.

477. _____. Thirty Studies in Swing. Enlarged edition.
      New York: David Gornston, 1945, 1965; copyright
      assigned 1970 to Sam Fox Publishing Co., Inc.,
      New York, 32 p.
      High school level. Published for treble and bass
clef instruments. Contains thirty-eight studies in many styles
of dance music; most emphasize syncopation. Suggestions
on interpretation and style are given, but instructional comments on rhythm and counting aids are lacking.

478. _____; Harry Huffnagle; and David Gornston.
      Forty Rhythm Etudes. Enlarged edition. New
      York: Pace Music Co., 1949, 1966; copyright
      assigned 1970 to Sam Fox Publishing Co., Inc.,
      New York, 28 p.
      High school level. Published for treble clef instru-
ments. Contains forty-seven syncopation studies in the progressive jazz style. No instructional comments or counting
aids are given.

479. Paulson, Joseph. Get in Rhythm. Westbury, NY:
      Pro Art Publications, Inc., 1948, 31 p.
      Junior high--high school level. Published for all band
and orchestral instruments with piano-conductor score. Contains forty-four unison studies and fifteen fully orchestrated compositions dealing with the following: common time rhythms,
march rhythms, waltz rhythms, eighth-note rhythms, fox-trot
rhythms, dotted-eighth rhythms, tango rhythms, rumba rhythms,
bolero rhythms, and "five-quarter" rhythms. Music from the
standard literature is used, but sources of much of the material
are omitted; such identification, if included, might lead to increased learning and interest on the part of the student. Ictus
marks are indicated in the unison studies as counting aids. Supplementary material includes a page of major scales, a chart of

relative note values, and twenty-four one-line, non-pitched
rhythm patterns to be used for testing or auditions.

480. Prescott, Gerald R. The Magic of Tempos. Melville,
      NY: Belwin Mills Publishing Corp. , 1959, stu-
      dent's book 32 p. , conductor's score 60 p.
      Junior high--high school level. Published for all
band instruments with condensed score. Reveals to students
an immediate use of various rhythms and serves as an introduction to the vast range of rhythmic and melodic forms in
music literature.
      The book is organized in sections dealing with spe-
cific meter signatures: marches, gavottes, schottisches,
hornpipes, fox-trots, and tangos are presented as examples
of 4/4 meter; marches, polkas, galops, and habaneras are
given as examples of 2/4 meter; mazurkas, waltzes, min-
uets, and boleros are included as 3/4 meter; 6/8 meter
presents marches, barcarolles, jigs, and reels; and ¢ meter
includes marches, cakewalks, boogies [sic], rhumbas, congas,
and beguines.
      As each form is introduced, a paragraph of in-
terest regarding the form is given. Then follows
appropriate selections putting these various forms
to use. In order to perform these arrangements
with ease, the basic rhythm structure of each
form is first presented in a unison preparatory
exercise. --Foreword.

481. Steiner, Eric. Tuneful Rhythm Patterns. Melville,
      NY: Belwin Mills Publishing Corp. , 1956, 24 p.
      Elementary--junior high school level. Eighteen ar-
rangements for piano, some adapted from the standard literature, designed to strengthen the student's rhythmic feeling.
Each arrangement is constructed from one repeated rhythmic
pattern and has an amusing title whose words fit the rhythm.

482. Stuart, Walter. Lessons in Rhythm and Syncopation.
      New York: Charles Colin, 1960, 17 p.
      High school--college level. Published for treble
clef instruments. Contains 167 short exercises arranged
progressively in order of difficulty using syncopated rhythmic
patterns in the modern jazz style. Meter content is limited
to 4/4, 3/4, and 2/4. Ictus marks are employed as counting aids.

483. Yaus, Grover C. Division of Measure. Melville,
      NY: Belwin Mills Publishing Corp. , 1965, 16 p.

Elementary--junior high school level. Published
for all band instruments with piano-conductor score. Contains thirty studies in progressive order consisting of rhythmic and rest patterns, scales, and staccato passages. Each
study ends with a well known melody which is often rhythmically quite different from the rhythms encountered in the
first part of the study. No counting aids or instructional
comments are given.

484. _____. Fifty-Four Harmonized Rest Patterns.
         Melville, NY: Belwin Mills Publishing Corp.,
         1954, conductor's score 48 p.
         Elementary--junior high school level. Published
for band instruments with piano-conductor score. Presents
an interesting, game-like approach to rhythmic counting and
performance. It is designed to be used by beginning students
who have an ability to play elementary rhythm patterns. Consists of familiar melodies, broken into short solo sections
and assigned as solo parts to various instruments. The solo
parts are not marked as such in the students' books; each
solo part is preceded by various rest patterns termed "harmonized rest patterns." In order to reconstruct the broken
melodies, each student must count his rest patterns correctly
and play his solo part with rhythmic precision.

485. _____. Forty Rhythmical Studies. Melville, NY:
         Belwin Mills Publishing Corp., 1958, conductor's
         score 43 p.
         Junior high--high school level. Published for all
band instruments with piano-conductor score. Contains unison studies from two to four lines in length written in traditional 19th-century exercise style. Each study drills one or
two rhythmic patterns. Students should have previous knowledge of rhythmic patterns as no instructional comments or
counting aids are supplied.

486. _____. One Hundred and One Rhythmic Rest Pat-
         terns. Melville, NY: Belwin Mills Publishing
         Corp., 1953, 21 p.
         Elementary--junior high school level. Published
for band and orchestral instruments with piano-conductor
score. Contains 101 short unison studies emphasizing rest
patterns. The book is designed to develop students' ability
to count rests as well as note values. No counting aids are
included.

487. _____. One Hundred and Twenty-Seven Original

Exercises. Melville, NY: Belwin Mills Publishing
Corp. , 1956, 23 p.
Junior high--high school level. Published for band
and orchestral instruments with piano-conductor score. Designed as a continuation of One Hundred and Fifty Original
Exercises (No. 490), it is written on the same plan. However, new rhythmic patterns are introduced at a faster rate.

488. _____. Thirty-Two "All in One" Studies. Melville,
        NY: Belwin Mills Publishing Corp. , 1960, 21 p.
Junior high--high school level. Published for all
band instruments with piano-conductor score. Each study is
in unison and contains a slow, slurred section, a section of
staccato rhythmic patterns, and section consisting of a variety
of scales, rest and rhythm patterns, arpeggios, and meter
changes. No counting aids are employed.

489. _____. Twenty Rhythmical Studies. Melville, NY:
        Belwin Mills Publishing Corp. , 1952, 21 p.
High school level. Published for all band instruments with piano-conductor score. Useful as an extension of
the Forty Rhythmical Studies (No. 485). Contains twenty
studies consisting of original, unison melodies which introduce
different rhythmic patterns in a somewhat random order. Unlike the Forty Rhythmical Studies, it attempts to keep the
student constantly on the alert. Rhythmic sequences are sud-
denly broken; syncopated patterns are introduced unexpectedly.
No instructional comments or counting aids are given. The
student must have good technical facility and physical endur-
ance to play the studies as they are a page in length and
contain very few rests.

490. _____ and Roy M. Miller. One Hundred and Fifty
        Original Exercises. Melville, NY: Belwin Mills
        Publishing Corp. , 1944, 30 p.
Elementary--junior high school level. Published
for band and orchestral instruments with piano-conductor
score. Contains 100 progressive rhythmic patterns, thirty-
three scale exercises, and twelve warm-up exercises in unison, and five harmonized tune-up exercises. The melodic
content is primarily in exercise style, utilizing scale frag-
ments. No counting aids are given; instructional comments
are almost entirely lacking.

APPENDIX

GALIN'S CHRONOMERIST

The following table compiled by Pierre Galin (1786-1821) is found in Émile Chevé's The Theory of Music, translated by George W. Bullen, 2nd ed. (London: Moffatt & Paige, 18??), pp. 69-70. It represents the fundamental approach used to teach rhythmic subdivisions of the unit in the Galin-Paris-Chevé school. The syllables under the notes, often called "French time-names," were added by Aimé Paris and have had a great influence on more recent approaches, such as that of Zoltán Kodály. In this table, the subdivision of the unit is not continued beyond quarters, sixths, and ninths and does not include rests.

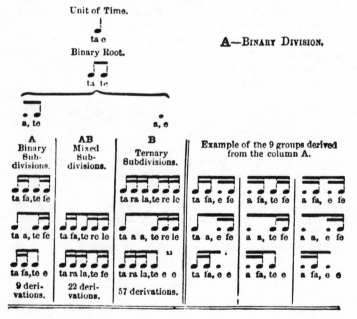

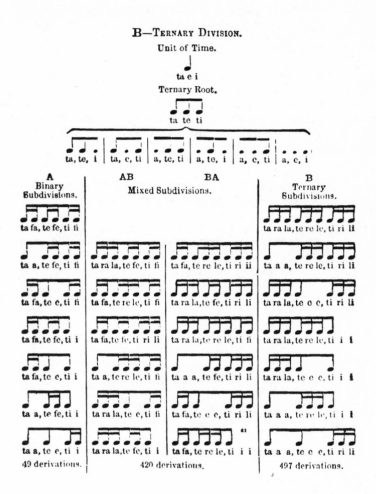

On pages 70-71, Chevé explains the basic mechanics
of the time-names proposed by Paris:

> As all the subdivisions of the unit result from the
> binary and ternary roots, Aimé Paris adopts the
> two vowels A and E to express halves, and the
> three vowels A, E, I,* to express thirds, and in
> such a manner that, in a binary group, A always
> denotes the first half and E the second, while in

*Pronounced <u>ah</u>, <u>ay</u>, <u>ee</u>.

a ternary group, A always denotes the first third,
E the second, and I the third third. The sound I
is, therefore, peculiar to the ternary root, while
A and E are common to both.

To distinguish an articulate sound from a prolongation, Aimé Paris adopts the T, which he joins to a
vowel to express an artciulate [sic] sound, while he
employs the vowel only for a prolongation. The silence or rest he calls CHU, and the prolongation of
a rest he calls U.

. . . .

To express the first binary subdivision, he uses
the two articulations T and F, . . .

. . . .

To express the first ternary subdivision, he uses
the three articulations, T, R, L, . . .

INDEX OF AUTHORS, EDITORS, AND REVIEWERS

69974

WINICK, STEVEN
  RHYTHM.

DATE DUE

GAYLORD   PRINTED IN U.S.A.